THE COMPASSIONATE MIND

THE COMPASSIONATE MIND

Theological Dialog with the Educated

Donald L. Deffner

Publishing House
St. Louis

3558 S. Jefferson Avenue, St. Louis, MO 63118-3968
Manufactured in the United States of America

Library of Congress Cataloging-in-Publication Data

Deffner, Donald L.
The compassionate mind: theological dialog with the educated/
Donald L. Deffner.
p. cm.—(Concordia scholarship today)
Includes bibliograhical references.
ISBN 0-570-04543-6
1. Apologetics—20th century. I. Title II. Series.
BT1102.D36 1990
269′.2—dc20 90-31367

1 2 3 4 5 6 7 8 9 10 99 98 97 96 95 94 93 92 91 90

TO
Dr. Arthur J. Manske
Kalamazoo, Michigan
who encouraged me
along the way
in the halls of Academe

The Church, when it turns to the educated, is not compromising its mission responsibility by concentrating on an unimportant minority of the American citizenry. . . . They constitute an integral part of the American population. If the Church fails to bring the Gospel to these people, it shall fail to speak to America itself.

—Joel H. Nederhood

Contents

Foreword

The Concordia Scholarship Today series explores current issues from a theological point of view and suggests how the household of faith may meet the challenges to its self-understanding and self-image that come from the surrounding culture. The hope is that we "may be able to comprehend [more fully] with all the saints what is the [extent of] the love of God" toward all his creatures (Eph. 3:17–18).

While all the volumes in the CST series offer new insights, some are largely theoretical with a minimum of direct application. *The Compassionate Mind,* growing out of classroom and pastoral experience, suggests how others might be helped to "comprehend the love of Christ." The author maintains that discussing literature—almost of every kind—offers a natural setting for gaining rapport with the educated. While he cites primarily works from an earlier decade that were helpful in his campus and seminary ministry, he urges the reader to examine current literature with which the educated may be familiar as a springboard for profitable theological dialog.

Openness to broad discussion is highly important because the educated, according to the author's definition, are not only those who have completed formal education but all who have learned to integrate their background with what they have learned, as they wrestle with the persistent questions of life. Conversely, some with formal training have not faced the basic issues and have not understood fundamental Biblical principles, the fallen nature of the world and human beings, the redemption by Jesus Christ, and, despite the lingering taintedness of human nature, the infinite possibilities that the redemption offers for coping with, even enjoying, life as the Spirit transforms and guides thinking Christians.

Instead of offering "recipes" for evangelization, the author provides settings and ideas to show that everything has theological implications, presenting "natural" opportunities for witnessing. The CST series encourages Christians to think theologically about all matters of life. Salutary suggestions for sharing the Christian vision are offered as a basis for further exploration. Though some may prefer pat answers, two people may opt for quite different *applications* of non-negotiable Biblical principles. The distinction between doctrine and practice must always be kept clear. When Biblical principles do not demand a given response, and when the implications and applications of Christian theology are justifiably debatable, then Christians need to be open to different opinions and also to later revisions of their own. Because human perception, will, and reason have been impaired since the Fall, the Christian must be ready to admit error in judgment even when firmly convinced of the decision at the time. Therefore, free and open discussion should continue; and binding decisions on the application of Biblical principles should be avoided.

In any case, Christians must respond. Exploration of the issues must grow out of reliable study and research of the Scriptures and of every other related, legitimate field of study. The net result may not yield theological applications that markedly differ from the past, but the value of such study lies in the learning process and in the assurance that the issue has been properly addressed.

Your comments and opinions on this volume and others are invited.

The Publisher

Preface

This book is intended for all who are serious in their Spirit-led desire to carry out the Great Commission to the whole world, especially to the so-called "educated." My long association with students, working with them in campus ministry, has affected the perspective of this study, but the focus is on the educated, both with and without a formal education. An objective I had in mind while compiling this study was to help Christian apologists gain a better understanding of the educated so that they might more easily take steps to reach them with the Gospel.

An underlying objective throughout is to sensitize the educated people of the congregation and community, to help them think theologically (because nothing is secular—certainly not for the Christian), and to equip the educated for sharing the Christian message with others.

Finally, this writing is intended for the evangelization committee and even the entire congregation as they confront the educated with the message of their salvation through Christ Jesus.

The author gratefully acknowledges permission to quote excerpts from *The Cardinal Sins* by Andrew Greeley (1987), used by permission of Warner Books, Inc., New York, New York.

For contributions to or critical comments on the manuscript I am indebted to: David Owren, John Gerlach, Richard French, Ed Schmidt, Heino Kadai, Jeffrey Walther, numerous students and campus pastors, and, for a superb job at the computer, Sally Williams.

Special thanks go to my former colleague Wilbert Rosin and to other staff members at Concordia Publishing House for numerous helpful additions and suggestions.

Introduction

"You will move out of this area immediately!" The riot policeman meant business, and I moved. I was on Telegraph Avenue in Berkeley that spring of 1971. Students around the University of California campus were demonstrating again as they had so often done in the sixties.

One block away was the People's Park. Another block away was University Lutheran Chapel which I had served as campus pastor from 1947 to 1959. I remembered another chilling mob scene in 1959 when I watched ten thousand students milling around sorority row on a muggy spring night engaged in a panty raid.

Generalizations come easily about the moods on campus: the so-called *silent generation* of the stable fifties; the political upheaval of the turbulent sixties; the sexual revolution of the seventies; the *me* generation of the eighties and nineties (the Yuppies and Dinks).

But such over-generalizations ought to be suspect. Some theologians in the early eighties said the "signpost to the new theology" is now *indifference*, that the modern person's ennui or lack of curiosity about God's very existence—let alone the questions it might raise—is the starting point for rebuilding true Christianity.

But was that such a new insight? I remember a student in 1959 who thought he had a dialog going with an agnostic friend who was reading his copy of Albert Camus's *The Fall* until the friend said, "You know, Lloyd, I'm not really as interested as you think I am." And my philosophy prof at Cal in the early fifties blandly observed, "Is the question 'Is there a meaning and purpose in life?' a relevant question?"

The new (?) *me* generation holds that selfishness is a virtue. The universe must be understood rationally, and the individual person is God. And they told me over thirty years ago that Ayn Rand's philosophy wouldn't last. I remember her character John Galt saying in *Atlas Shrugged*, "I swear—by my life and my love of it—that I will never live for the sake of another man, nor ask another man to live for mine."

At the same time, the altruism of those who were concerned about societal change in the sixties persists into the nineties among those involved in the sanctuary movement or aid for the oppressed in South Africa and Third World countries. Would that more of the current *me* generation could be re-oriented towards "loving our neighbor as ourselves" as our Lord directed!—yet also seeing him as the source of such self-abnegation.

An 82-year-old Orthodox layman in Switzerland once told me the two most important things in life are modesty and a good death. That twofold insight continues to intrigue me. The first deals with our need for an absence of pride (*self*); the second with the crucial questions with which we need to cope:

—Who am I?

—Why am I here?

—To what should I commit myself?

—How shall I face my time to die?[1]

I believe that human beings have not changed all that much through history. The technology has changed, yes. But humanity is the same as in the Golden Age of Greece 2500 years ago, *curvatus in se*, curved in on one's *self*. Humanity is still in need of the gracious God who, in the Person of the Son, denied *self*, giving up the glory of heaven for the gore of the cross, dying for the sins of the world.

Nor has the mission of the church changed over the centuries. Christ's climactic final charge to his disciples in Luke 24:47 still remains: the message about repentance *to* the forgiveness of sins must be preached to all nations.

This study focuses on how that mission call may be better implemented, specifically with reference to the educated. The academic odyssey that led to this book began for me with the course Communicating with Adults at Pacific Lutheran Theological Seminary in the spring of 1959 while I was campus pastor in Berkeley. From 1959 to 1969 the journey continued in the course Reaching the Educated Adult at Concordia Seminary, St. Louis, MO (in correlation with the courses The Campus Ministry and Theology and Modern Literature). From 1969 to 1987 the quest returned to Berkeley and included students from Pacific Lutheran Theological Seminary and a variety of denominations represented in the Graduate Theological Union.

As I perused the collected stacks of student papers from twenty-eight years of classes, several themes emerged, among them the repeated quest for *a compassionate mind* to reach the *educated adult,* not a condescending mind, but a mind as Christ himself had, who "beholding him, loved him." (Mark 10:23)

This student refrain was reinforced in the textbooks selected for the course. For example, Joel H. Nederhood said we have little difficulty in feeling compassion for the poor and downtrodden. But we are not naturally sensitive to the poverty of the educated. What we need is the compassion Christ himself evinced in determining how we can most effectively approach the educated "who have deprived themselves of God's greatest grace."[2]

Anthony T. Padovano masterfully echoed such compassion, noting that our love for the educated should serve no utilitarian purpose. "In a sense, love must be useless to be genuine."[3]

J. B. Phillips wrote about two worlds of good will—"the one whose compassion and love flow out of its faith in God, and the other which produces actions of compassion and self-giving service with little or no articulate religious faith."[4]

Such compassion-apart-from-Christ came through strikingly in our study of the work of Albert Camus. Tobina Dalton, a former student of mine, in a paper for class, contended that "only by saying no to the official pieties of the age could Camus sustain and enlarge that compassion he had come to believe in as the 'redeemed' condition of man." But R. W. B. Lewis concludes that "there is yet too much mind in [Camus] for the compassion to do its full work in creating or restoring a believable image of man."[5]

However, the source and motivation for empathy for a humanity groaning in travail (only partially recognized, if at all, by contemporary writers) is not ourselves. Rather, we are driven back to the gospels again and again to meet the Master and Source of the compassionate mind. There, as we experience the faith which was once delivered to the saints and the great cloud of witnesses of Biblical history, we feel the brush of angels' wings as we meet our Lord himself in his sacred Word. My students and I repeatedly experienced that over the years.

I invite you to join me now on this collegial pilgrimage and enjoy a theological adventure such as the students and I did in Reaching the Educated Adult. It's geared for you, whoever you are, whether or not you are formally in the classoom.

* * * * * * * * * * * * *

The Setting for Reaching the Educated Adult

It might be helpful to picture the environment in which the students of my classes aired their ideas.

The classroom is a "clean, well-lighted place" with large windows, comfortable, carpeted, overlooking lush green lawns and towering pines. A hundred feet down the hillside is a Spanish modern building where there is hot coffee at the "break." To the east is Lake Tahoe, only three-and-one-half hours away, nestled in the snow-covered Sierras. Outside one bank of windows is a shaded patio with flowering camellias and from there a view to "The City"—San Francisco. The blood-orange arches of the Golden Gate Bridge shine in the radiant morning sun. Tiny white sailboats speckle the azure waters of the Bay.

Occasionally a deer wanders through the patio. There is the faint hum of traffic far below on the Bayshore Freeway. It is a good place to "come apart and rest awhile," for soon we must all go back down again—to the plain. But we must also study, for the Master has work for us to do.

I

ODYSSEY

1
Who Are the "Educated"?

Our Berkeley student congregation had gathered again for Sunday worship. I looked out over the assembly. About forty percent were visitors, with a sprinkling of international students. There were jocks and home economic majors, engineers and English Lit scholars, and a number of graduate students in physics and chemistry—a select audience.

These were people who had reached a certain intellectual and social level, hence needing special consideration as the church ministered to them.

Yet they were not an educated *group* or *class.* For their current educational experiences were quite different. Some spent their whole life buried in the natural sciences. They *thought* differently from other students. I remember some carrying around flash cards for two years trying to master the languages for the doctoral requirements in engineering. Some, brilliant scientifically but limited linguistically, didn't make it. Others specialized in the humanities, dealing with quite a different set of facts and asking quite different questions—ontological ones.

Joel H. Nederhood's description of the educated is helpful.[1] The *intellectuals* are the creative, original philosophers who mold the thinking of others. The questions these mental giants raise at a high level of thought and the answers they suggest ultimately filter down and affect those who ponder ideas—*the world of the mind.*

The *educated* are those—with or without a university education—who grapple with the great questions of life: who are you? where are you going? what is the meaning and purpose in life? They are critical thinkers, avid readers, keenly concerned about the world about them. Skeptical, existential, alert, they examine issues and make decisions with careful discrimination. Note that this includes those whose occupation is dull—e.g., insurance clerk, forklift operator—but who have pursued truth through private study, creative thinking, reading novels and intellectually oriented journals. The *uneducated educated* are the *technicians.* They are specialists in a particular task, but "that's it." Often lacking exposure to the arts or the humanities, some may be brilliant at the keyboard of a computer but quite immature otherwise.

One particular person comes to mind, a graduate student in chemistry. His adviser gave notice, "You be in this lab seven days a week—yes, Sundays included—or I'll drop you as my candidate." He was there!—and he earned his Ph.D. But he couldn't make decisions concerning his emotional life. The secretary of our student congregation was in love with him, and they dated each other. But as the months went by he just couldn't decide. In precomputer lingo it was "all slipstick but no lipstick." In desperation she and her mother gave him until January first to pop the question. The deadline came and went without a decision. So she married the next president of our congregation.

Make no mistake, technicians are not hopeless. Trained but not educated, and extremely narrow in outlook, most can be potential thinkers. And they too can grapple with the issues raised by the Gospel, more readily than those who have never been trained to study.

Our task, then, is to examine the profile of the persons before us. Autonomous and nonconformist, many are dominated by a scientific and secular worldview, nourishing deep-seated prejudices and misinterpretations about the Christian faith. They have wrapped a coat of mail around themselves, seemingly impervious to our message. Our mission is to lay bare the radical vitality of the Gospel.

But it must be done with *compassion.*

Without knowledge of literature pure theology cannot at all endure, just as heretofore, when letters have declined and lain prostrate, theology, too, has wretchedly fallen and lain prostrate; nay, I see that there has never been a great revelation of the Word of God unless He has first prepared the way by the rise and prosperity of languages and letters, as though they were John the Baptists. . . . Certainly it is my desire that there shall be as many poets and rhetoricians as possible, because I see that by these studies, as by no other means, people are wonderfully fitted for the grasping of sacred truth and for handling it skillfully and happily. . . . Therefore I beg of you that at my request (if that has any weight) you will urge your young people to be diligent in the study of poetry and rhetoric.

MARTIN LUTHER

From an illustration in *This Day,* March 1963, p. 12. Martin Luther, "Letter to Eoban Hess, March 29, 1523," *Luther's Correspondence,* trans. and ed. by Preserved Smith and Charles M. Jacobs (United Lutheran Publication House, 1918), II, pp. 176–77.

2

Books to Make Us Think

A colleague of mine was amused recently when a seminary student who had not majored in the humanities in college was asked to assess the collection of books in a library reference room.

"My! There are sure a lot of old books in there!" was the substance of the student's report.

I have always been somewhat amused by students who speak of "outdated materials." That annual challenge from students and the proliferation of books and knowledge in our day keeps all of us in academe on our toes. But the latest novel reviewed in *Time* magazine may not be the author's best one. John Updike, I feel, has not surpassed his masterful *Rabbit, Run* published in 1960. I know of a discussion group in San Diego which will not consider a novel until the author has been dead for five years and his work has stood the test of literary criticism. Literature classes still study *The Trial* by Kafka and *The Stranger* by Camus. I use the Bible a good deal—and it's been around for some millenia. I offer no apologies for my choices, though some may prefer to discuss only the most recent literature and only the best known authors and titles. The selections here serve our purposes very well, and the principles and concepts we will be discussing are readily transferable.

Everyone's approach to bibliographical resources is eclectic. We begin with a book that was a natural for our *compassionate* concern for the *educated.* To my knowledge this book, with its particular theme and format, is one of a kind.

Joel H. Nederhood, *The Church's Mission to the Educated American* [1]

Here is a study of major importance, not only for campus and town-gown pastors but for community-serving pastors as well.

The focus is on the church's responsibility to discover and respond to the thought world of educated people. The author begins with an excellent chapter on the New Testament church as *mission*, understood as that which occurs "when the church, which has been created a testimony to Jesus Christ, comes in contact with the world. If it is truly Christ's, it is *living out the spirit which he has sent.*"

Chapter two treats the church as mission in America. It notes that the contemporary expression of the church in our country is continually threatened by massive social forces. In the next two chapters Nederhood spells out the steps in approaching the "unconverted educated." First, we should know as much as possible about them. That requires distinguishing the *trained* from the *educated* products of our colleges; properly assessing the secular faith inculcated by so many "halls of ivy"; evaluating the breathtaking progress in the natural sciences and its effect on contemporary man; and looking with jaundiced eye at the religious language symbols used by the "educated," similar to Christian terminology, but with an antithetical frame of reference. Therefore, says Nederhood, "A missionary may never take communication with an educated individual for granted."

Next, we need to be aware of the misunderstandings and prejudices of the educated. Failure to distinguish between *organization* and *organism* colors the view of the church held by many college graduates who have taken too seriously their courses, for example, in descriptive sociology. The psychological approach to religion is similarly devastating for the educated person's evaluation of Christianity.

The college graduate is quite likely to believe that the Dead Sea Scrolls undermine the structure of Christianity, that "theology is a massive systematization of personal opinion and fantasy," and that the church is anti-intellectual and hypocritical. Such mistaken notions must be taken into account in describing the *unconverted educated.* Nederhood points out the substitutes for Christianity that often appeal to the educated, such as the exotic religions, liberal Judaism, and the new humanism. He vividly sketches the effects of modern literature upon contemporary man; secular images of man are interlaced through the reams that are cranked out by our modern "merchants of despair," the "futilitarians."

In chapter five Nederhood becomes specific about approaching the educated. He notes the current favorable social position of the

American church for reaching the educated and stresses congregational responsibility for mobilizing the mission. His primary concern is that "the local church recognize its worship service, in which the Word is preached, as the most important component within its mission approach to the educated .... No contact with educated people should be judged complete until attendance upon the preaching of the Word results."[2]

Nederhood clearly delineates basic content he wants in the message: (a) the God of Christianity is the Creator of the cosmos; (b) the Gospel demands decision in the light of the imminent judgment; (c) the Christian faith has implications for all of life. No author can be expected to treat his subject exhaustively to our satisfaction. Nederhood is no exception. Discussion offers the opportunity to spell out absolutely essential Biblical perspectives and supply correctives that dare not be overlooked: the broken relationship with God resulting from the fall into sin, justification through the redemption and resurrection of Jesus Christ, and the role of the Holy Spirit in regeneration and sanctification.

But all that Nederhood does say is consonant with the analogy of the faith. Happily he affirms that salvation is God's gracious gift (*sola gratia*), and, citing Berkouwer, describes election to salvation briefly as having "nothing to do with sinister arbitrariness .... The electing purpose of God opens the way of salvation, in which men learn that the salvation of God is only received as a divine *gift* and never as ... a way of *works*."[3]

In summary, Nederhood says the church must change its present relationship with the educated into a mission relationship. The tragedy is that many churches who are now attracting the educated are not proclaiming the Gospel. Instead, they are trying to be "successful." They should live deeply in the Word of God and proclaim this Word with assurance and boldness.[4]

Nederhood's book is a powerful contribution. His stress upon the distinction between church as organization and as organism (the institution in contrast to the mystical body with Christ as its head) is of profound significance in our dialog with non-Christians.

An even more important insight is that many educated erroneously interpret Christianity; they understand the Church's terminology and proclamation in the light of their own misinterpretations of Christian doctrine. Therefore, "A missionary may never take communication with an educated individual for granted."[5]

Indeed, the *apparent* familiarity with Christian doctrine should be a red flag to Christian communicators, alerting us to expect serious misunderstanding of the commonly used Christian terms.[6]

And the real task for us is a *massive dismantling process*. Only after the accumulated misconceptions about Christianity (as distinguished from church as an institution) have been eliminated can fruitful dialog occur with the educated. This often requires inspecting and removing each false understanding of Christian doctrine and then rebuilding the Biblical structure of Christian truth piece by piece (when the opportunity is there, for example, in an adult instruction course).

Dogmatism or boldness? Nederhood draws attention to the dilemma:

> The prejudice of the educated against the dogmatic spirit of the Church puts the Church in a difficult position because the very nature of the gospel demands that it be presented in a straightforward, unequivocal way; it must be *proclaimed*. However, because of what "dogmatic" has come to mean (e.g., doctoral, doctrinaire, opinionated, bigoted, unreasonable, arrogant), the Church may never admit that its message is dogmatic. At the same time, the Church must understand that the educated can hardly avoid thinking of the Church's proclaimed message as being dogmatic.[7]

For the characteristic message of the early church, and ours, "the *way*, the *manner* was this:

> the message was spoken with boldness (*parresia*). It is only in terms of this boldness that the Church can make the proper adjustment to the educateds' hatred of dogmatism.
>
> When the message of the Church is marked by this boldness, the educated, when taking offense, actually take offense to the gospel itself and to the power of Christ which is expressed when the gospel is proclaimed in this characteristically Christian manner . . . .
>
> It is important for the Church to remember that it continually stands in danger of exchanging this peculiarly Christian boldness for an ordinary dogmatism.[8]

Questions remain. Are Nederhood's descriptions of the educated and their rejection of Christianity characteristic of all humanity? How does the *skandalon* of the Gospel relate to this issue? Nederhood makes meager reference to the Sacraments and the role of the church in society. Nevertheless, he provided helpful insights often overlooked in the literature on evangelization. Nederhood's challenge stands:

> But when the Church turns to the educated, it engages in mission activity which demands that the Church muster all its spiritual resources. The message will have to be a pure one, and it will have to be as true as incisive, sanctified theological reflection upon the Biblical givens can make it. And the message will have to be proclaimed by individuals who are highly qualified men who are willing to work at understanding the needs of educated people and who will be able to sense at once the particular emphases in the Scriptures which must be stressed in order that the educated may be brought to repentance and faith. Only the church at its best can be truly mission, and only such a church and such a mission can be expected to make an impact upon educated people.[9]

Anthony T. Padovano, *The Estranged God: Modern Man's Search for Belief*[10]

Anthony T. Padovano's writing was particularly helpful in evaluating key writers who influence the thought-world of the educated.

Padovano deals with the questions, Who is modern man? Who is God (as the Catholic Church understands him)? and How should God be presented to modern man?

Padovano's first topic is "Existentialism and Religious Belief: the Mood of the Age is Set." Then follow seven-to-ten-page summaries of the thought of five key philosophers. These with the encapsulations of the literary figures that follow are alone worth the price of the book. Padovano treats Jean-Paul Sartre, Martin Heidegger, Karl Jaspers, Soren Kierkegaard, and Gabriel Marcel.

In 1966 when he wrote Padovano concluded that the trend of philosophical thought was that (1) science must not be worshipped; (2) the real issues are God, death, conscience, time, and selfhood; (3) concern with freedom; (4) the twentieth century person is desperately searching for love and personal communication; (5) today's thought bears constant reference to transcendence.

Holding that Christianity preaches a *transcendence* beyond reason and that *Being* "has a human face and a gentle heart," he concludes,

> Our task today then is to understand the men we must reach. We must show we can identify with those who do not know who they are, who feel the terrible cross of uncertainty about life's meaning, those for whom God is not life and salvation but a question mark. We too must be modern men who see a broken and tragic world—men who have no final answer but preach a Way.[11]

Convinced that "every effective insight into man's nature brings one to God," Padovano considers those who write "enduring literature." He provides insightful summaries of Fyodor Dostoevsky, Thomas Wolfe, Franz Kafka, Albert Camus, J. D. Salinger, William Golding, and George Orwell. Padovano comments,

> The most hopeful thing about modern man is the fact that he cares and that he sees himself and his science as not enough. We may not have found the Way and yet we seem to be on the right road.[12]

Subsequently Padovano asserts that "modern man not only seeks but fears some genuine values," and presents a Christian proposal. He assesses the reactions of Dag Hammarskjold and Ingmar Bergman to problems under the headings of love, freedom and God:

> The former grows in belief and devotion as he solves the problem of human love. The latter is tormented because his concept of God is a threatening one.[13]

The Catholic Church, in responding to the problem of God's existence, has made but four statements: there is a knowable God; he possesses some attributes which we can realize; he is a God able to know; he is a God of concern, choice, and love.

In addressing how God should be presented to modern man Padovano affirms that

> God must be presented in evident terms of who he is, but also in terms of our age's need for him. A God who is infinite can be presented to finite men in an infinite number of ways without fear of compromising God's identity. A God who is ageless can

be presented differently in every age and yet not become another god in the process.[14]

Padovano concludes with statements about God that might be useful in presenting him to contemporaries:

> God is the One who gives man the divine
> God is the One who gives man the human
> God is the One who gives man freedom
> God is the One who gives man Christ
> God is the One who gives man personhood.[15]

Padovano's final plea is that his book go beyond a mere theological undertaking. He sees theology as a call to prayer and worship, that a person might be chastened by humility and fired by love.[16]

Padovano's book became a major resource and foil for discussion in the course in ensuing years. We contrasted his Thomism with Protestant Biblical theology and examined current intellectual trends to answer the question he asked in 1966: "Where is our philosophical thought taking us today?"[17] Many of his insights have lasting value. His succinct sketches of selected philosophers and literary artists are superb.

He also shows a strong note of compassion when dealing with the contemporary person's fear of love:

> We must give of ourselves to another, to share with the other our joy and interest, understanding and knowledge, humor and sadness, weakness and strength. In the process of giving of ourselves to the other, we must develop a sense of concern for the other's life and growth, a sense of care that makes me my brother's keeper—a sense of respect so deep that I never exploit him and so selfless that I never want him to be what I want him to be but rather what he must be. And so I encounter the other and in our effort together we discover ourselves. In love, I discover myself; we discover both of us; and if the love is genuine and deep, I discover all men and God through this experience. If ever we really love one person, we love all persons, the entire world, the experience of life, every man, and God himself. This love is built on our need of each other. Today I; tomorrow you. Though we need the other and meet the other, our love or friendship or fraternity serves no utilitarian purpose. In a sense, love must be useless to be genuine.[18]

"Love must be useless to be genuine!"

The ongoing tension of faith vs. "unfaith" received particular attention in Padovano's work. In discussing Kierkegaard, he stated: "We can even accept the fact (with him) that a person who has passion in his atheism may be closer to God than one who toys with theism as an hypothesis."[19]

This question, how close or how far this person is from God, became an intrinsic part of the assignment students pursued as they chose a character from a novel or a play and sought to dialog with the individual with the ultimate desire to present the Gospel.

In *Death of a Salesman* was Willy Loman very close to or very far from God? Did Holden Caulfield in *Catcher in the Rye* need more Law or Gospel if you were in conversation with him? In *Rabbit, Run*, even though the Lutheran minister blasted Harry Angstrom with judgment, wasn't his approach *at that point* more fitting than the bland ineptitude of Rev. Eccles? And what is the contact point with Meursault in *The Stranger* or J. B. Clamence in *The Fall*?

How would one respond to Albert Camus himself if you were to dialog with him in person? Camus claimed his works were *not* autobiographical. But he tellingly raises in his work the age-old question, How can a loving God let the innocent suffer? And the question threads its way through *The Estranged God*.

Padovano picks up the difficulty of faith in Dostoevsky: "Faith never fully overcomes the temptation to unfaith; nor does atheism fully overcome the tendency to faith."[20]

Padovano quotes Ivan in *Karamazov*:

> What is surprising . . . is not that God should really exist; the marvel is that such an idea, the idea of the necessity of God could enter the head of such a savage, vicious beast as man. It is such a touching, holy, wise idea and does man so much honor.[21]

But atheist Dr. Rieux in Camus's *The Plague* is not convinced.[22] A child has just died from the plague in terrible agony. Father Paneloux agrees with Rieux's feeling of mad revolt at the death. "It passes our human understanding," he says. "But perhaps we should love what we cannot understand."[23]

But Rieux responds, "Until my dying day I shall refuse to accept a scheme of things in which children are put to torture. I resolved to have no truck with anything which, directly or indirectly . . . brings death to anyone or justifies others putting him to death."[24]

And Rieux tells Tarrou, "Since the order of the world is shaped by death, mightn't it be better for God if we refuse to believe in Him and struggle with all our might against death, without raising our eyes toward the heaven where He sits in silence."[25]

Padovano provides a helpful beginning point for the Christian in response to Dr. Rieux.

> We affirm God because He is there and because we were made for Him. We affirm Him because without God we cannot fully be ourselves or totally love each other. Aquinas shows well this fact that God is an end in Himself when he says that those who deny God's existence because of evil in the world are given but one reply: "But I am Who I am." Beyond all our syllogisms and problems, God exists. And He will not be forever silent or forever still. He is Who is and man cannot declare Him dead. Therefore we must say to our fellow men: Weep not for God but for ourselves if God is dead. To those who say God is dead, we answer that God is living and we say this not really for the sake of God but for the sake of man.[26]

Anthony Gibson picks up this theme in his *The Silence of God: Creative Response to the Films of Ingmar Bergman*.[27]

Gibson feels God is operative and communicative throughout Bergman's films. "Their theme is truly the silence *of* God, not merely the silence that provides there is no God there."[28]

For the Christian, then, absence of evidence is not evidence of absence. Luther would say that *Deus absconditus* is *Deus revelatus*, known to us because he is revealed in Scripture and understandable to fallen man because of Jesus Christ. And the response to "Where is God now?" is not only to say, "Here He is—He is hanging here on this gallows."[29]. . .

but to point beyond those gallows
to the cross
where His son hung
in our place.

Bishop Hans Lilje clung to that Christ. He had been condemned to death because of his anti-Nazi stance during World War II. I heard him speak in 1952 at Grace Cathedral in San Francisco. He spelled out "The Fall" of our age, and how he had personally gone through

The Valley of the Shadow (his book). He said the guard told him in his cell, "When I hang you I will kick out the stool from under your feet and walk away and no one will hear your last, gasping breath."

And yet, Lilje affirmed, he continued in hope and affirmed that in the face of everything "this is the Springtime of the church."

And it is the springtime for our renewed and refreshed dialog with the educated, to tell them again about *The God Who Is There: Speaking Historic Christianity into the 20th Century*.[30]

John Powell, *A Reason to Live! A Reason to Die!*[31]

John Powell warmly engages the reader in the search for "some middle ground of free air and open-mindedness between the pressures of indoctrination and the prejudice of rebellion."

He holds that "our ideas of God, faith, church have been built upon a limited experience by a limited understanding."[32] Such a premature conclusion bears re-examination, and again the "dismantling process" is in order. Many of the educated have rejected a God who has never existed. As R. W. B. Lewis wrote, "The God whom Camus, following Nietzsche, has declared dead was a God who in fact had not been alive very long."[33]

What is needed is for the educated to meet for the first time "God's kind of God," the true God revealed in the compassionate Suffering Servant, Jesus Christ.

Powell ably introduces this God to the searcher with an open mind. Obviously his 1972 assessment of our technocratic culture needs updating,[34] but many of his insights have lasting significance.

Note especially

- his analysis of "the deepest human damage of our day . . . self-alienation" (38ff.);
- his brilliant antinomies of traditional faith vs. the mood and view of modern man (69ff.);
- a new image of God looking with delight upon a "good world" (80–83);
- the beginning of faith: The external word of God (92) and the internal word of God (102);
- faith in contrast to belief (108);

- his views on prayer (114, 117ff.); especially cf. "The Art of Prayer" (134–450142);
- the tests distinguishing genuine from illusory religious experience (121–122);
- the places to encounter God (123ff.);
- the tension between "Show me, and I'll believe" and "Believe in me, and I'll show you" (130 ff.);
- the "wrath of God" (170);
- knowing *about* Jesus and *knowing* Jesus (178 ff.); and
- the delightful modern paraphrase of the story of the Prodigal Son (184 ff.).

I believe Powell's *A Reason to Live!—A Reason to Die!* has continuing value as a basic textbook in understanding and reaching the educated adult.

C. S. Lewis

C. S. Lewis' writings are, of course, *the* prime resource for reaching the educated adult. Note the columns listing his works—and studies about him—in *Books in Print* so many years since his death. Because of the abundance of available literature on this Christian literary giant, extended treatment of his work here is unnecessary. His *Case for Christianity* is *the* book to put into the hands of the honest agnostic. It is part of *Mere Christianity*.[35] Later, when the timing is right, give your doubting friend *The Screwtape Letters*.[36]

A fine videotape, entitled *Shadowlands*, gives a warm insight into Lewis' character and philosophy, particularly with respect to his marriage to a woman who was formerly a Marxist and an agnostic.

Also worth noting are *Through Joy and Beyond*, a video;[37] and Kenneth C. Harper's D. Min. thesis, "C. S. Lewis as a Paradigm of Pastoral Apologetics."[38]

J. B. Phillips

Sadly, few of J. B. Phillips' books are in print today, but they deserve careful reconsideration. In my opinion his classic little volume *Plain Christianity*[39] is still one of the best introductory books for the "average" searcher considering the Christian faith. But that should be followed with *God Our Contemporary*.[40]

It addresses the intellectual, including both the "dead wood" in the English churches and the "good persons of unfaith" on the outside. Many of his insights readily apply to our task of reaching the educated adult today. Note his perceptive comments on "*Christian* humanism" (24), the limitations of science (chap. five), the need to cope with the evil endemic in humanity (40), the challenge to confront Christ (52–53), and the varied routes to Christian faith (112ff.)

Phillips assesses why "the whole language, teaching, and climate of 'Church' appears almost totally irrelevant to modern life."[41] He points to the hereditary indoctrination of many Christians, the inadequate training of ministers and their almost total incapacity to comprehend and interact with non-Christian ways of thinking. He observes that many pastors have never had secular experience in the contemporary world and thus fail to understand the perplexity and insecurity of godless materialism. That has happily changed somewhat in the last generation. Far more seminaries today include second career people; the average entering age is closer to thirty—quite a contrast to the former twenty-three-year-old from a Christian college who majored in religious studies.

But do today's pastors fully understand the world of unfaith? It is this tragedy—and barrier between the good persons of faith and the good persons of unfaith—that Phillips probes so masterfully.[42]

Phillips, in his proposal for spiritual renewal, repeatedly stresses *Christian* humanism:

> The Englishman may be suspicious of churchiness, of technical religious terms, of rites and robes, of bells and smells, which seem to him irrelevant to the business of living. But he is by no means unmoved by the needs of the handicapped and underprivileged, the homeless and the helpless, when he is made aware of them. It seems to me there that the most hopeful place in which to build a bridge between the worlds of faith and unfaith is on the common ground of human compassion.[43]

"Let there become one army of true goodness and true love," he urges, following the Spirit of the contemporary God. The church should welcome the searcher; and the persons of good will but little faith should invade the churches. Christians must seriously attempt to lead Christian lives. And agnostics are challenged to test the truth of the Christian faith and commit themselves to the struggle.[44] For then they will know the splendor of the truth as Christ's words are fulfilled.

> Whoever is willing to do what God wants will know whether what I teach comes from God or whether I speak on my own authority.[45]

While discussing Phillips or any of the writers mentioned here, sooner or later it becomes obvious that, while their observations are usually consistent with Biblical truth, they frequently leave gaps that ought to be filled. The whole of Christian doctrine cannot be spelled out in every writing, but it must always reflect a clear understanding of the Fall, the redemption, justification, sanctification, and other essentials of the faith.

Chad Walsh

Chad Walsh's excellent text *Campus Gods on Trial*[46] provided the grist for many exciting discussions in both courses I taught, Reaching the Educated Adult and The Campus Ministry.

Walsh describes his own spiritual odyssey:

> While attending little Marion College of the United Lutheran Church I was exposed to the doctrine of justification by faith but fancied myself an atheist and delighted in missing chapel. But I was tracked down by Jesus Christ and was baptized after joining the Beloit College faculty. The Christianity I accept is one that is classical, Christ-centered, resting on the doctrines of the Incarnation, Atonement and Resurrection. As a rector in the Episcopal Church and a professor of English I live in two worlds. The latter position enables me to keep in close touch with what students are thinking and what they are writing.[47]

Walsh defines an intellectual as "one who thinks because thoughts are worth thinking. The intellectual can put his thought into words, express and defend them rationally. He lives in the realm of ideas."[48]

Walsh's book has had wide use by campus pastors, as a springboard for "nod-to-God" weeks (religious emphasis weeks) and as a college text. In the original edition in 1952 he noted that the college campus was not godless at all, but was rather overpopulated with progress, materialism, scientism, humanitarianism, relativism, and security. It is of historical significance to compare his changed assessment of the academic deities when he revised and enlarged his book in 1962. At that point he added nihilism, libertinism, idealism, skepticism, and others to the list. And it is intriguing to gauge, as we have noted, which of these "isms" are perennial and which are uniquely "new" today.

Walsh's writing is engaging and includes firsthand interviews with students and much rich illustrative material. After examining atmospheric, psychological, heartfelt, Christian, and unChristian reasons for not being a Christian, he includes a most helpful guide to those willing to begin the journey and wanting to "fit the jigsaw puzzle together."[49]

Here and there I do not share his theology, but Walsh's volume is well worth re-discovering. Note especially

- on Christianity's being "wish-fulfillment" (42);
- on the origin of evil (96);
- on science vs. scientism (53);
- on hypocrites in the church (110); and
- on God being on trial (111-115).

For the "me-generation" committed to autonomy and non-conformity, Walsh's *Campus Gods on Trial* presents a ringing challenge:

> And here is the mystery and the paradox. The person who uses his freedom to give his "I" into the hands of God, there to be remade in the image of Christ, is really only lending it. For God gives it back. One day, when you least expect it, he returns it to you, much improved from the scrubbing and alterations it has received. What began as surrender to a master ends as sonship to a father.[50]

William E. Diehl

William E. Diehl's *Christianity and Real Life*[51] is of special help to educated Christians in the business world. Some students also felt it was one of the best books on the role of the laity.

I often introduced Diehl's book with a survey on business ethics and the clergy. The survey posed the question, How much guidance did your church and clergyman provide for ethical problems you and your associates faced in the last five years? Interestingly, 35 percent said "None;" 25 percent, "Some, but not enough;" "16 percent, "About the right amount;" and 23 percent, "Can't say."

According to Donald W. Shriver, Jr., of North Carolina State University, lack of communication is the problem. The business person sees the clergy as living in a world of mere ideas; never meeting a payroll; engrossed in ancient history; using a theological language that no one else understands; and apt to be strangely critical of the American way of life.

And the clergy person sees the business person as unaware of the role of ideas in the person's own business activities; careless about the past and anxious about the future; using a hard-to-understand economic language; and likely to be uncritical of the American way of life.

Low-key discussions between pastors and business persons may begin to breach the barriers and resolve ethical conflicts, and Diehl's book could be an excellent text for an adult study group to explore the problems facing people in the business world. Discussion topics could include

- The social activist who was criticized because "a true Christian is a peacemaker in the community, not a troublemaker" (4);
- Most of our programs are geared to people "coming in" not "going out." (13) [I suggest we actually should have a *Servants' Entrance* sign inside the church exit];
- Many church leaders assume and Diehl questions that "the faithful will just naturally find the effective means for relating their faith to the outside world" (18); (Don't we trust the intellectual and spiritual capacity of the laity? Cf. also p. 39);
- "The pastor sees his chief responsibility to be the preservation of the congregation as an ongoing group" (30);
- (Quoting Peter Berger): "The most common delusion in this area is the conviction of ministers that what they preach on Sunday has a direct influence on what their listeners do on Monday" (34). Diehl comments, "The sermon, as we now know it, is not at all an effective way of encouraging and supporting laypeople's ministries in life" (36). Summing up the opinions of some contractors, he states: "The church does not know how to speak the eternal truth of the gospel in a way that can be understood and appropriated by modern industrialized man" (82);
- "How does a layperson initiate a discussion relating to his faith

without immediately turning off the other person?" (35); (My comment is that it's not always "Jesus at the water cooler");

- The necessary shift from the laity as *objects of formation* to the laity as *subjects of their own formation* (40); "acting as their own agents, there must be more development of unofficial Christian communities apart from the ecclesiastical structure" (97);
- The aid-man style of [lay] ministry—identification of gifts, development of skills, support groups (54, 84);
- Contrasting styles of [lay] ministry (57);
- Seed-dropping (64–65);
- The lay person and current theology (70–71);
- "House-churches"—their elements of support, small size, and need-meeting with flexibility (100–103); and
- Worship as a focal point for spiritually equipping laity (109 ff.).

J. Russell Hale

J.. Russell Hale's exploratory study, *The Unchurched: Who They Are and Why They Stay Away*,[52] is widely quoted in the literature on evangelization.[53]

Hale spent a month in each of six "irreligious" counties in the United States and interviewed 165 people. His categories depicting the motives people have for deciding not to return to the church include the anti-institutionalists; the boxed-in, the burned-out, the cop-outs (later changed to "floaters"), the happy hedonists, the locked-out, the nomads, the pilgrims, the publicans, the scandalized, the true unbelievers, and the uncertain. Once in a conversation I had with Hale he expanded on the need for "active listening" to these people. "Your tone of voice, gestures, etc. are very important as you say, 'I'd like to have you tell me your story about what you think of the church. Go back to your childhood.' *And they really open up*."

"If you listen when they tell you their story, a point will come when they'll say, 'Tell me your story.' And you don't hand out tracts, but as the two stories converge there is in the miracle of dialog the point when *God's story* can come out."

So we need to be sensitive to the vulnerabilities of people and await that precious moment when the "rumor of angels" impinges on their ordinary experiences.

But if these people come back into the church, noted Hale, *the climate of acceptance is crucial* so that they will stay.[54]

Hale said his category of the anti-institutionalists was largest—those who see the church as preoccupied with self-maintenance and who object to its political nature. They see its emphasis on finances, buildings, and property.

His category of "the true unbelievers" was the smallest, and the number of people in this group in the United States has not changed much in the last forty years. Up to 94 percent of people being interviewed today say they do believe in "God." For the mood in our culture is against being an atheist. But then again, some interviewers observe, people often lie in their responses to questions!

Nevertheless, Hale says he found few authentic unbelievers in his sample. In his language, there were not as many "village atheists" around as are alleged, but he might have found more, he suggested, had his sample been selectively drawn from academe.

Hale subdivides this type into three: (1) *Agnostics/Atheists* "deny the existence of any such ultimate reality as God or hold that such reality is unknown or unknowable."[55] Typically, Hale comments, "Both these questions are meaningless: Who am I? Why am I?" I was particularly intrigued by his reference to an 86-year-old man in Sarasota, Fla., who explained his agnosticism by saying he was "still waiting for all the facts to come in."[56]

2) "The *Deists/Rationalists* comprise those whose theology, whether formally or informally articulated, is based on human reason rather than revelation."[57]

3) The *Humanists/Secularists* stress self-realization through reason without benefit of anything supernatural. Many are also happy hedonists. The church is meaningless. "I don't think religiously. God-talk is superfluous." But Hale observes that "their commitments to justice and love may parallel that of the Christian church member."[58]

Hale told me in 1987 that the prototypical Orange County secularist is the one to watch, as indicative of where our country is going.

If he were to start over again, he would like to study the searching adult. He particularly recommended reading Lesslie Newbigin,

Foolishness to the Greeks: The Gospel and Western Culture;[59] Helmut Thielecke, *How to Believe Again*;[60] and Helmut Thielecke, *Nihilism: Its Origin and Nature with the Christian Answer*.[61]

Edward A. Rauff

Edward A. Rauff did a follow-up study of Hale in *Why People Join the Church*.[62] He lists the following reasons that people come into the church: the influence of Christian people; family relationships and responsibilities; the search for community; personal crisis; a feeling of emptiness; the end of rebellion; the journey toward truth; the response to evangelism; the reaction to guilt and fear; God's *kairos* (appropriate time); church visit, program, special event, sacred act; and the influence of pastors.

Of all these, friends or relatives were most frequently the influence and source of evangelization.[63]

Especially significant for us is Rauff's "journey toward truth" category and his comments that are singular to our task. Although the social, familial, or mystical aspects of the church presumably were ignored or at least subordinated to solid, logical conviction by this rational/intellectual type, "some of the interviewers related their experiences *with great emotion*."[64]

In evangelizing the educated, not "just a rational mind" but the whole person with *feelings* and emotional sensitivities calls for attention.

Study the data (118–129) and listen to Bonnie's story as she sat in the park writing Are-you-there? type poems to God. Though attracted to the church *by the liturgy* and the charismatic movement, she met with obstacles when she attended. "The churches didn't want to talk with me."[65]

I was especially fascinated by the odyssey of Danielle, a highly intelligent, articulate woman of Jewish background. In Nederhood's phrase, she discovered the *organism behind the organization* that was the church.

> I began to realize that the popular Christianity that I had always heard around me had absolutely nothing to do with Christianity at all.
>
> The *New York Times* I have problems with. The New Testament I don't.[66]

She even saw through "Cecil B. DeMille Christianity."

> But even with all of that junk in there, the center of it, God sacrificing himself in that way, I guess that was the first thing that drew me to it. The enormity of that act. That, I think, is still the center of my faith. The fact is that that cross is the center of the faith.[67]

She was particularly drawn to C. S. Lewis and other people whose lives were testimonies to Christ—"signposts on the way to someone's Baptism."[68]

But like Bonnie, although she found a Lutheran congregation that she visited to be very nourishing spiritually, she explained:

> Having to deal with people within the Church, whom I wouldn't be caught dead dealing with outside of the Church, has also been a good experience. It's been very painful. It's been a part of that death that the New Testament talks about. I find that it's murder to really see and cope with people that drive you through the wall. But I wouldn't give up the experience. I think this mountain-top religion is useless and being in a congregation is a good place to at least start, you know, with the idea that, "Well, if Christ loves them, I guess I can at least make some small attempt to deal with them."[69]

This calls to mind the Irish ditty: "To live above with the saints we love, ah, that is the purest glory; to live below with the saints we know, ah, that is another story."

Or as Sheldon Vanauken says in *A Severe Mercy*,

> The best argument for Christianity is Christians; their joy, their certainty, their completeness. But the strongest argument *against* Christianity is also Christians—when they are somber and joyless, when they are self-righteous and smug in complacent consecration, when they are narrow and repressive, then Christianity dies a thousand deaths.[70]

Note Rauff's account of Jack's journey: "I had to go in through the Bible."[71] That prompts us to ask, "How do we get the educated into the Scriptures?" Suzannah "came in" through a Christian type of prayer-discipline. Note Paul's sudden realization that Christ "was the one—after all!" (much like the beginning of chapter 31, *The Screwtape Letters*) and the conclusion to his long journey:

> Corporate Christianity is critical to our Christian experience.

> You can't have the opportunity to be with other believers if you're locked away in a prison. But for believers who have the opportunity to be with others, it's critical. The whole New Testament concerns the church. To live your life apart from other believers, apart from a church, is denying God's plan.[72]

And Paul stresses the need for outreach and "body life" rather than "Sunday Christianity."

> What Christ is really working for in this particular age is not great heroes but a corporate witness—Christians who love one another and yield to one another and share one another's burdens . . . And I'm growing up because of my experience with other Christians—the life we have here.[73]

You can't be a Christian in a vacuum.

Richard Lischer

I recommend Richard Lischer's *Speaking of Jesus: Finding the Words for Witness,*[74] written for laypeople, for reaching both the general public and the educated. His theology is sound.[75] He focuses on the people of God gathered around Word and Sacrament.

> Evangelism is the community itself radiating light and warmth from an energy source hidden deep within its midst.[76]

Lischer's intent is not to devise a strategy for building bigger churches nor even for recouping losses. He speaks of a "lesser commissioning" which (1) instead of trying to win the world focuses on a narrower, congregational scope; (2) takes the possibility of rejection seriously; and (3) suggests following Jesus' own method of sending out witnessing partners.[77]

Rehearsed words are exchanged for the methodological nakedness of only bearing the authority of Christ. And Christ's pattern is carefully followed. (1) It was *dialogic*. He listened and did not use others' questions as springboards for his own premeditated answers. (2) His communication was *holistic*. He forgave and healed. (3) His approach was *situational*. He went where the people were. (4) His communication was in *simple*, "secular" language. (5) He called his listeners to *decision*. "Follow *me*," he said.[78]

Next Lischer ably analyzes the reasons that evangelism in a parish becomes ineffective or nonexistent. He then focuses on *story*—the stories "that Christians speak to non-Christians in order to call forth repentance, faith and discipleship." Of particular help are pages 38–48 where Lischer presents a masterful summary of salvation history. Some of my students have declared it the best encapsulation of "God's story" they have ever encountered.

Excuses follow for refusing the message and disowning the story. Lischer concludes with helpful resources, principles, strategies and a bibliography for Christian communication.

Lischer's book is of particular help because of its scholarly clarity and its faithfulness to the Biblical model of evangelization. Lischer appropriately denounces the oxymoron "anonymous Christian" which some faddists use to describe the "secret, submerged belief of all who, though explicitly rejecting Jesus, live lives of mercy, justice, peace, and hope."[78] He respects the integrity of honest agnostics and takes their unbelief seriously without whitewashing it as "anonymous Christianity."

He does not get bogged down with intellectual objections to the Christian faith. "The evangelist should not become so involved in reasoning through the intellectual arguments that he or she forsakes the personal, warm witness to the truth that surpasses human understanding."[79]

In short, Lischer affirms, "the evangelist brings a ministry of compassion."[80]

Additional Resources

Emory A. Griffin's *The Mind Changers*[81] is a humorous approach on how *not* to evangelize—The Non-Lover, The Seducer, The Rapist, The Smother Lover, The Legalistic Lover, The True Lover.

Edward F. Markquart's course ***Witnesses for Christ: Training for Intentional Witnessing***[82] does not encourage "doorbelling," calling on strangers, home visits to new members, or any formalized type of evangelism. Rather, it concentrates on helping people verbalize the faith within already existing natural relationships.

Evangelization: Mission Trends #2[83] is a standard work, a classic collection of monographs covering the global and multicultural mission of the church, written by John R. W. Stott, Renè Padilla, Hans-Ruedi Weber, Kosuke Koyama, Martin E. Marty, W. A.

Visser 't Hooft, Manas Buthelezi, and others. Cf. also the other paperbacks in the series.

Representative comments worth noting include the following:

> The Great Awakenings, the revivals of the 19th century, the surge in church membership that followed World War II, and the continuing growth of Christianity on university campuses stemmed not from grand designs, elaborate structures, and expensive programs, but from the work of the Holy Spirit in individual congregations, obscure pastors, small prayer meetings and local gatherings of concerned believers (Deane A. Kemper, 133).
>
> There is no mention whether the word that was "evangelized" was believed, or whether the inhabitants of the towns and villages "evangelized" were converted. To "evangelize" in Biblical usage does not mean to win converts (as it usually does when we use the word) but simply to announce the Good News, irrespective of the results (John R. Stott, 9–10).
>
> "What will happen if we plan our evangelism project according to the insights we have now gained?" they asked. "Frankly," Hans Ruedi Weber replied, "it may be that many among your present church membership will leave the church and that a few who are now completely outside the church will join you."
>
> "You mean to say that as a result of this project we may in the end actually be fewer!" they asked in astonishment.
>
> The answer was yes. "The result of true evangelism may be the cutting down of the number of church members" (64–65).
>
> Most N.T. letters to younger churches contain neither exhortations to organize evangelism campaigns nor methods of increasing numbers. These letters are *prefaces to martyrdom*, and mission is there not connected with statistics, but with *sacrifice*. Consequently, the deepest reason for Paul's apostolic joy was not his and the younger churches' success, but the conformity to Christ's suffering in the fulfillment of their ministry (Hans-Ruedi Weber, 66).

Erwin J. Kolb provides practical helps on personal witnessing in his book ***A Witness Primer***.[84] Like Rauff, he stresses the need to work through natural relationships in presenting Christ to those outside the body of Christ. Study and action questions conclude each chapter and a helpful annotated bibliography is included.

Robert Kolb in ***Speaking the Gospel Today***[85] treats basic doctrines in relation to the mission of the church.

Morris Watkins, *The Great Commission*.[86]

Rebecca M. Pippert, *Out of the Salt Shaker: Evangelism as a Way of Life*.[87] Evangelization as a life-style. A warm, human and "vulnerable" guide to both relaxedness and authentic enthusiasm in conversational evangelism. A valuable annotated bibliography: understanding the Christian faith; evangelization Bible studies; books for Christians on better witnessing; and in-depth books on issues for non-Christians.

David G. Truemper and Frederick A. Niedner, Jr., *Keeping the Faith: A Guide to the Christian Message*.[88] "A commentary on the catechism designed to help Christians tend the faith they hold, nurturing their understanding of it in our changing age. It interprets Christian doctrine as instruction on how to bear the message well, how to tell the story in such a way that Christ is glorified and sinners hear the good news."

Terry K. Dittmer, ed., *Wings of Faith: The Doctrines of the Lutheran Church for Teens*.[89] Written for youth (which also include many "educated") but highly valuable for later age levels as well. Excellent chapters by William Weinrich, John Johnson, David Lumpp, Dean Wenthe, Paul Raabe, and Terry Dittmer.

A Summary Look at the Educated

The educated constitute a significant and integral part of the population. They are the "thinkers," the decision makers, and power brokers who have achieved a certain cultural, intellectual and social level that requires the church's special attention in its evangelization activities.

The educated are whole persons with deep human needs, not just intellects. They have often wrapped a "coat of mail" around themselves that resists the Gospel. The influence of science upon them and their harbored prejudices and misinterpretations of Christianity bear careful evaluation by the Christian communicator.

Approaching the educated must be marked by boldness without dogmatism, authority without authoritarianism. Above all, the Christian is compassionate and humble rather than clever, while learning the art of loving listening.

The Christian communicator enters the thought-world of the educated keenly aware of one's own fecklessness and frequent imperviousness to the Gospel. The apologist knows that in dialog both are utterly dependent on the "crazy, holy grace" of God. And as their trust relationship develops, their mutual challenge in getting to know Christ better is to have the experience "of a God madly in love with us, and then live as one must who is caught up in such a love affair" (Andrew Greeley).

The odyssey continues. We have commented on some of the key textbooks used in the course *Reaching the Educated Adult.* In addition, secular literature became a major resource for understanding the mind of the educated. It became a stimulating crucible for interacting with the ontological questions of the educated.

And so we return to our odyssey of a generation ago. For many of the educated (as Walter Cronkite used to conclude his newscast) "that's the way it was."

3

Modern Literature and the Educated

In Acts 17:28 the Apostle Paul quoted contemporary literature to the educated of his day with the phrase "as even some of your poets have said." Luther called for the study of poetry and rhetoric, going so far as to claim that "without knowledge of literature pure theology cannot at all endure." A mentor of mine, Dr. Gerhard Lenski, son of the famous Bible commentator R. H. C. Lenski, first turned me on to the theological significance of contemporary secular literature. Holding up a copy of Albert Camus's *The Fall* in class, he eyed me and said, "Ah, Deffner, this is a great book!" Until then in my early campus ministry I had always thought my job was to continue studying, preach sermons, make calls, and counsel. But Lenski opened the door to the broad world of theology and modern literature. Later it even led to a series of courses that students teasingly dubbed "Deffner's Dirty Books."

But the door was open. And studying the prophetic voices in modern fiction became a major source for understanding the world of the educated and for sensing where modern culture was heading.

This chapter assesses the significance of literature as one medium for better understanding the educated.[1] Following that the "compassionate mind" of Albert Camus is explored as a prime example of the new humanism of many of the educated today.

The chapter concludes with two examples of Christian fiction.

Portraits of Humanity in Modern Literature

To understand the educated so that we might better reach them with the Gospel, we do well to listen to their spokespersons. A. L. Kershaw points out the need to listen to the perceptive spirits among the contemporary poets, novelists, playwrights, artists, and composers of the day, who, he avers, "have been far more sensitive to the judgment of God on the hollowness of our life and society than have the majority of religious leaders."[2]

Furthermore, a whole spate of books has appeared in recent decades analyzing the contemporary images of humanity found in literature and drama, in addition often affirming that the novelist or dramatist is giving us a more realistic picture of people than do most clergy or theologians. Such authors include Nathan A. Scott, Jr., Amos N. Wilder, Stanley Romaine Hopper, William R. Mueller, among others.

For the purposes of this study we cite the somewhat representative thesis of William R. Mueller in *The Prophetic Voice in Modern Fiction.*[3] This writer criticizes the mass of contemporary literature that professes to be religious but fails to qualify as either great literature or profound religious thought.

> There is much pulp devoted to the mawkish expression of man's love for God, just as there is to man's love for woman. Much "religious" writing is sentimental; it titillates flabby and easily seduced emotions and offends the taste of anyone with either literary or religious sensibilities.[4]

He affirms that a Dante or a Milton would be unlikely in our century since Biblical situations and vocabulary have been overworked and sentimentalized by superficial and inept artificers. To be effective any serious writer must resort to the portrayal of different situations and the use of a different vocabulary.

> In short, there is the paradoxical situation in which much of our ostensibly religious writing is hardly worth the time of a person seeking religious insights or aesthetic satisfaction, and in which the most profound religious writing is frequently to be found in works that may initially appear to have little or nothing to do with man's relationship with God.[5]

Although Mueller feels that we find humanity's condition nowhere more expertly diagnosed than in the pages of today's perceptive novelists, he does not conclude that the individual in search of one's self and God can now "lay aside his Bible and confidently turn for the revelatory and redeeming Word to the words of James Joyce or Albert Camus.[6] But in modern fiction the serious student may find affirmations regarding humanity that are forcefully set forth and have previously gone unnoticed. Biblical truths regarding humanity may come home in a startling and penetrating manner through the medium of drama or fiction.

> The novelist will not save us, but he may well bring us to the knowledge that we are in need of salvation.[7]

The images of an individual have been compared to the four tines of a pitchfork. The one is the real, "inside" me. Another is the me I think I am—my mask to the world. A third is the self I would like to be. And there is the final self I ought to be. The authors of some of the previously mentioned books contend that much preaching and religious writing is more often concerned with the last three tines of the pitchfork than with the first, while the imaginative secular literature of our time shows us as we really are.

Stated positively, a minimum contribution of much modern literature consists in portraying humanity in desperate need of salvation. The popular image of humanity today is a person swimming in three feet of water, casually interested in a nearby boat. At any time the individual can stand up and walk to shore. But the voices of modern fiction are presenting humanity as struggling in thirty feet of water, and reaching the boat is a matter of life and death. One is trapped and needs some kind of salvation. But the wailing voices disagree on what the boat is—or indeed, whether there is any boat in sight at all.

The personality types described, of course, are not clear cut. They interplay and merge with one another. Readers may differ as they categorize the types. Furthermore, the works cited—some outstanding and some not—simply serve as examples. While they may not contribute to Christian growth, they help by depicting humanity more clearly to us.

These literary images impinge upon the thinking of the educated, many of whom are avid readers. To a great extent, they, too, are what they read. Identifying with the hero or the heroine, as is often done by the reader, subtly leads to rationalizing and sanctioning of acts and points of view portrayed in the plot. The following are some of the portraits of humanity that appear in modern literature.

The Person of Complacency

The person of complacency is coddled with creature comforts, preserved by piety, pills, and psychiatry.[8] "Generous Electric" company has become the god of the apathetic or unconcerned person.

> For multitudes among us there is no vision of a City of God coming down from the skies, such as appeared to the author of the book of Revelation. They have a vision of a vast conjuring trick coming up from the earth, from the mines and the factories—a paradise of chromium and ceramics, egg-shaped automobiles and layer-cake houses, skyscrapers made of glass, and clothing made of soybeans. They do not need a Day of the Lord; the General Motors will take care of all that![9]

Here is the breakdown of human values. The machine and the organization replace the rich human relationships of acceptance, affection, and love.

The complacent individual is not directly the subject of an extensive literature, for this person is essentially self-satisfied. However, the life of the falsely secure individual is not all bliss. Burt F. Coody describes the vague image one has of a "house of security."

> In it are the rooms of the organization, the vocation, the job, the family room, the living room of social status and entertainment, the den for comfort, relaxation, sports, the bedroom for sleep and sexual gratification. The foundation for the whole structure is money and social status provided by being a member of the "in-group." When these are removed the whole structure falls, and he is plunged into despair or defiance.[10]

Because this type of person is perhaps the most commonly known among us, a resulting complacency actually becomes deceptive, as Coody implies. For under the surface of the delicately structured life of the Yuppie in the three-piece suit may be a figure either of the emptiness and hollowness of life or of one ready to blast out against the world in torrents of hatred and anger.

The Person of Despair

It is not hard to hear the voice of the person of despair, for this lament is constantly being intoned by those writers whom Niebuhr called the merchants of despair—the futilitarians. This is the person futilely waiting for God (as some interpret it) in *Waiting for Godot*. And although the modern novel and drama which sketch this prototype often have no plot, suggesting that life itself has no plot or purpose, yet underneath it all we see the root of humanity's despair—an ineradicable and all-consuming self-love.

Luther had a phrase for it: *curvatus in se*—curved in toward oneself. If a hermetically sealed capsule of this year's "hit" albums were to be exhumed some centuries from now, the analysts would hear one recurrent theme in many variations as the egocentric person croons, "*I* want you." "*I* need you." "*I* miss you."

One is reminded immediately of Jean-Baptiste Clamence's classic comment,

> It is not true, after all, that I never loved. I conceived at least one great love in my life, of which I was always the object.[11]

Robert Fitch suggests that these writers make one think of a group of men on a ship at sea:

> They toss the pilot overboard, cast away the rudder, wreck the compass and the sextant, bash in a few bulkheads, splinter the decks—and then sit down in a chorus to lament that they are lost. . . . [Moreover] they insist that everyone must get into the same boat with them.[12]

An example of the person of despair is in Franz Kafka's *The Trial* in the frustrating, anxious, hopeless person who is brought to law but who never fully knows why he is being tried. The trial preparations drag on for months, but the individual finally realizes that there is only utter futility, that "it is futile to argue an innocence which does not exist and to look to oneself or any other human being for an acquittal which is not his to give."[13] The theme of despair in Kafka emerges even more poignantly in *The Castle* when a surveyor comes to a small village and asks people how to get to a certain castle where he is to perform some task. He finds that they only turn from him in fear and terror. Try as he might, the man cannot reach his goal. He never gets to the castle to find out what he was supposed to do. Critics disagree on the ultimate message of the book. Is it that one cannot by one's own strength reach God? Or is it that there is no real point to life, or if there is a meaning, is its purpose unclear?

Or read *No Exit* by existentialist Jean-Paul Sartre. In the brief

47 pages of the play, brilliantly written, Sartre paints the horrid, chilling picture of three wretched creatures imprisoned in a parlor "down under." One died a coward's death; another was guilty of infanticide; another methodically destroyed her closest associates in life. Moving to a dramatic climax, the truth finally breaks in on coward Garcin:

> So this is hell. I'd never have believed it. You remember all we were told about the torture chambers, the fire and brimstone, the "burning marl." Old wives' tales! There's no need for red-hot pokers. Hell is—other people![14]

As the three scratch and claw at each other and baby killer Estelle attempts to kill carping Inez with a paper knife, they finally realize that they are "dead already." They slump on their respective sofas, faces blanched. Laughter dies away, silence follows, and Garcin mutters, "Well, well, let's get on with it."[15]

Here Sartre has played out a powerful theme of chilling nihilism in a stark drama that literally breathes the philosophy of the "unalterable futility of it all."

Or look at a Broadway play made into a Hollywood film, *The Dark at the Top of the Stairs.*[16] Much of the play graphically depicts creatures of despair, inmates of prison cells of their own making. Selfish, unable to accept each other as they are, they eke out an existence of fractured relationships, and the house that they inhabit is not a home but is under a dark pall. The mood of the family is exemplified in the answer of the young boy. When asked why he fears the dark at the top of the stairs, he replies, "You can't see ahead."

The description of Helen Detweiler in Cozzen's novel is in the same vein.

> Close to Helen's consciousness, nearly impinging on it, was . . . the forbidden horror, the dreadful eyeless face of our existence. In desperation . . . Helen pushed back the horror; refused to look. On the world she never made, she imposed with all her strength a pattern of the world she wanted—a place of peace, of order, of security; a good and honest world; the abode of gentle people, who, kind-minded, fair-minded, clean-minded, remarked the perfect man and beheld the upright; and who, once believed into existence, could alleviate . . . Helen's recurrent anguish of

trying not to know, yet always knowing that in the midst of life we are in death.[17]

Other works illustrate the theme of despair, for example, Tennessee Williams' *Baby Doll*, the very different *Long Day's Journey into Night*, by O'Neill, and more. Repeatedly the characters are "trapped by the past, caught in the web of their own ignorance and egotism and incompetence, and so, by a kind of atheistic predestination, move on to their doom."[18] The real, added tragedy is that often spectators viewing these dramas or reading these books are not moved to compassion, but rather intensify their own egotism and self-pity.

For a final moving portrayal of the person of despair consider the pitiful Willy Loman in *Death of a Salesman*.[19] Willy wanted desperately to be loved and accepted by his family, but felt the only way he could achieve this "acceptance as is" was to "wow" them by being a big success. The shadowy figure Uncle Ben tells Willy that life is a jungle and you have to "be hard." For a moment in the play, Willy sees a glimmer of hope. Speaking of his son Biff, he says: "Isn't that—isn't that remarkable? Biff—he likes me!" But soon he is back on the squirrel-cage treadmill to "success" again, roaring off in a car into the night—and suicide.

And in the moving, staged funeral, at which the expected crowds never appeared, the family members puzzle over the untimely death. The wife, who made the last payment on the house that day and felt all Willy needed was "just a little more salary," wails her lament, "Why did you do it?" But Biff sums up the poignant epitaph of Willy Loman—and of the person of despair: "He never knew who he was!"[20]

The Person of Defiance

A third major literary portrait emerging from the tons of paperbacks stocking the bookstalls and the reams of print that go into the hits and flops of Broadway is the person of defiance.

Some may feel the prototype of this individual is implicit in the egocentric, keenly analytical pages of Philip Wylie's *Opus 21*. Others may point to the rambling "novels" of Jack Kerouac (*The Dharma Bums*, *On the Road*) some thirty years ago, although it is questionable whether such writing should be dignified by including it in a discussion of literature. Or browse through John Osborne's *Look Back in Anger*. Tom Driver, then drama critic for *The Christian Century*, described the blasts of venom and irrationality of this character we might just as aptly label "animalist": "He rants at her like a wounded adolescent, shrieking until the world shall listen to his story of pain, anger and unfocused frustration."[21] Here humanity is portrayed as incapable of love and reason. Here blatant degradation, the antithesis of God's intended purpose in the creation, is put forth.

The works of Tennessee Williams (*Suddenly Last Summer, Sweet Bird of Youth*) come to mind again. The ability of Williams as a playwright is beyond question. He describes the objective of his writing in the stage directions for *Sweet Bird of Youth*. It is to be a "snare for the truth of human experience." Elsewhere he describes the nonverbal or nonideational character of this dramatic expression of truth:

> The color, the grace and levitation, the structural pattern in motion, and quick interplay of live beings, suspended like fitful lightnings in a cloud, these things are the play, not words on paper, nor thoughts and ideas of an author, those shabby things snatched off basement counters at Gimbel's.[22]

And the ranting, defiant creature in many plays of Williams is a hideous Dorian Gray, whose portrayal has telling shock value. Fitch describes the colors on the canvas as the portrait comes into focus in *drama of defiance* of Williams in *Cat on a Hot Tin Roof*:

> The one irreducible value is life, which you must cling to as you can, and use for the pursuit of pleasure and power. The specific ends of life are sex and money. The great passions are lust and rapacity. . . . It is not a tragedy because it has not the dignity of a tragedy. The man who plays his role in it has on himself the marks of a total depravity. And as for the ultimate and irreducible value, life, that in the end is also a lie.[23]

A final example of the defiant person is seen in still another and quite different work, J. D. Salinger's epochal *The Catcher in the Rye*. I remember a twenty-five-cent (!) version of the first edition. But then sales of the book skyrocketed on campuses around the country as Salinger was "discovered."

Young Holden Caulfield has been kicked out of prep school

and spends a kaleidoscopic forty-eight hours in New York City. The portrait that emerges as he muses back on the life at school and soliloquizes on the strange events that transpire in the city, is both tragic and comical. But underneath is the bitter and sardonic current of defiance toward the artificial world around him.

For Holden, life seems a farce. Everyone is putting on a big act. They're all phonies, hypocrites—like the actors on the stage of Radio City Music Hall carrying crucifixes all over the place, who he feels really can't wait to get outside and take a drag on a cigarette.

The church and religion receive the jaundiced eye from Holden, too, especially the disciples of Christ.

> I'm sort of an atheist. I like Jesus and all, but I don't care too much for most of the other stuff in the Bible. Take the Disciples . . . while He was alive, they were about as much use to Him as a hole in the head. All they did was to keep letting Him down.[24]

Young Holden rambles on, lancing and scoring the sham and deceit of life around him. The only thing he would really like to be, he muses, is a "catcher in the rye." He imagines thousands of children playing in a rye field near a "crazy cliff." There's the chance some might run near the edge and Holden would be there to catch them.

> That's all I'd do all day. I'd just be the catcher in the rye and all. I know it's crazy, but that's the only thing I'd really like to be. I know it's crazy.[25]

Some critics have suggested the rather implausible analogy of a Christ figure in this brief vignette. More credibly one might see this defiant young man rejecting everyone around him as frauds and phonies and attempting to be his own savior or a (strange) type of self-styled savior for others.

Whatever the analogy, *Catcher* offers a vivid picture of a person of defiance.

We are not wandering from our task of understanding educated adults. Living in the fast-moving world of computers and with the demands of the corporation on their time, some may not be readers of literature as much as others. But we can still be sensitized to their world through the study of fiction. And we can resonate to the insight noted above, namely, that whatever mask the educated are currently wearing, when the two matchstick props of status or money are knocked away, the images of despair or defiance can readily appear.

Literature is, to repeat, a further insight into the thought-world of the educated because many *do* read voraciously. Just note what people are reading on airplanes. It's not *all* Danielle Steel. Further, I have seen a dully conducted adult class triple in membership in a suburban parish when "theology and literature" was announced as one of the topics in a new short-term, primary interest group. People who were nonattendants otherwise came out of the woodwork to attend the class, great interest was stirred, new friendships were formed, and follow-up discussion circles begun.

In another instance a pastor who took a course stressing the theological significance of modern literature began reading current novels and exclaimed to me: "My wife asked what I was reading, and we got to talking. I suddenly discovered the whole 'subculture' of the books she had on the headboard above our bed. I entered into a world which I did not know existed. Now we are communicating in a way we never did before!"

So, for many people, current literature can be a fruitful contact-point. This is particularly true with respect to books that relate to the next portrait to be discussed, the New Humanism.

The New Humanist

A fourth significant image in contemporary literature is that of the person who has faith in humanity in spite of all the things that cause complacency and despair and defiance in others. Nederhood singles out this type as a representative of what he calls the New Humanism.[26]

William Faulkner in his dramatic Nobel-prize acceptance speech spells out the tenets of this secular faith. He states that in our society today there is such a general and universal physical fear that for many the problems of the spirit no longer exist. The only question is, When will I be blown up? In this setting the poet—the literary artist—he feels, must realize that "the basest of all things is to be afraid." That fear one must "forget forever" and return to the "old verities and truths"—writing not of the glands but of the heart.

Unlike the merchants of despair, Faulkner declines to accept the end of humanity as inevitable. He feels that when the final ding-dong of doom has sounded, the last thing to be heard will not simply be "man's puny inexhaustible voice, still talking."

> I refuse to accept this. I believe that man will not merely endure: he will prevail. He is immortal, not because he alone among creatures has an inexhaustible voice, but because he has a soul, a spirit of compassion and sacrifice and endurance.[27]

It is the duty of the poet and the writer, Faulkner says, to write about these things. The artist's voice is not to be merely the record of humanity, but "it can be one of the props, the pillars to help him endure and prevail."[28]

Consonant with this virile and secular faith, but also in a class by himself, and presenting perhaps the greatest challenge to the Christian Gospel, is the "theology" and the person of Albert Camus. The portrait here displayed was not only put forth in his writings but was also lived out by this late French author, killed in an "absurd" automobile accident in early 1960 while speeding on his way to Paris. The uniqueness of Camus is that he rises above the despair and defiance of most prophetic voices, admits *nostra culpa* (our guilt), but clings firmly to a humanistic credo of hope in humanity despite life's ultimate absurdity, even while "professing vociferously his own infamy."

Camus is not a nihilist, nor an existentialist, nor an atheist—in the common sense of the terms. Rather he accepts the irrationality of life, going on to say,

> In the lowest depths of our nihilism, I have searched only for reasons to transcend it.... I believe I entertain a just notion of the greatness of Christianity. But there are some of us in this persecuted world who feel that if Christ died for certain men, He did not die for us. And at the same time we refuse to despair of man.... If we consent to do without God and without hope, we are not resigned to do without man.[29]

Proclaiming such a "faith," Jean-Baptiste Clamence steps forth as its protagonist in the autobiographical-confessional work of Camus, *The Fall*. It is the chilling story of a retired Parisian lawyer emoting to an acquaintance "on a bench out of the rain" beside the canals of Amsterdam. "The Fall" of this masterful man, as the story spins out, was his ultimate, ghastly realization that he was a hypocrite par excellence, a fraud-hero of the first rank. The dream of his supreme dominance and intrinsic worth as an exceptional person was shattered by a series of circumstances that revealed the true nature of his inner infamy. He speaks of "keeping people in the refrigerator," bringing them out, and using them when best it suits him. He even had the luck of having membership in the Legion of Honor offered to him two or three times and of experiencing the privilege of turning it down!

> I am not hardhearted, far from it—full of pity, on the contrary, and with a ready tear to boot. Only, my emotional impulses always turn toward me, my feelings of pity concern me. It is not true, after all, that I never loved. I conceived at least one great love in my life, of which I was always the object.[30]

But the grisly confession, though it admits personal guilt, subtly shifts over to the self-centered guilt of us all.[31] And when the very thought of redemption flickers to mind, he muses,

> "O young woman, throw yourself into the water again so that I may a second time have the chance of saving both of us!" A second time, eh, what a risky suggestion! Just suppose, *cher maitre*, that we should be taken literally? We'd have to go through with it. Brr . . . ! The water's so cold! But let's not worry! It's too late now. It will always be too late. Fortunately![32]

This is the voice of the *New Humanism*. After repeated, horrendous world conflict and unparalleled brutality, a not-so-thin voice still remains—not only enduring but prevailing and calling for renewed hope in humanity without God.

Other Portraits

There are other images in the literature of today of which we might speak.[33] We could make out the scientific person, committed to the ideology of scientism as a *modus vivendi*. We could see a neurotic person, a compartmentalized person, or the isolated person. We could outline the bewildered person in the midst of computerized, specialized society, overwhelmed by the complexity of modern existence and wondering which way to turn. Or again there is the determinist person created by Communist ideology or depth psychology, who indulges in a sense of self-justification and abdication of responsibility: "I *had* to do this." "Something or someone did this *to* me." "I cannot do other than what I have done."

Running through many of these portraits is the interplaying image of the person of anxiety. W. H. Auden spoke of the inhabitants (or inmates?) of the "age of anxiety," "children lost in a haunted wood." And the frenetic bankruptcy of humanity's hopes is expressed in a similar vein in A. E. Houseman's *Collected Poems*:

> And how am I to face the odds
> Of man's bedevilment and God's?
> I, a stranger and afraid,
> In a world I never made.[34]

Interpretation and Criticism

In retrospect several points should be kept in mind in interpreting this literature.

First of all, from the Christian perspective, the question should always be asked as to whether the writer portrays the true nature of humanity. Does the artist depict people as more base than they are, as no more than animals? Or, conversely, is humanity depicted as better than it really is in its depraved state after the Fall?

Basic is the Biblical teaching that sins (plural) are the result of sin (singular).

A true perspective will reflect the Biblical view that God's perfect creation was ruined by the Fall into sin. Few people will deny the innate moral weakness of humanity, which the Biblical student recognizes as the result of what theologians have come to call *original sin.* Sins (plural) and subsequent results of sins (problems, burdens, trials) ultimately stem from original sin that has been passed on and has affected all humanity ever since, spreading its runners everywhere. Christ has paid the penalty for sin. The penitent Christian sinner therefore may be forgiven the sin(s) he has committed and empowered by the Holy Spirit to lead a more sanctified life.

Second, the reader should remember that the novelist's "law diagnosis" is not to be equated with the full Law of God found in Scripture. Secular literature knows only the "law affirmation" of humanity's entrapment. God's Law, his demand for perfect righteousness and holiness, must be spelled out. That must, of course, be countered by the lively "good news" that through Christ God has "reconciled all humanity to himself" (2 Cor. 5:19) so that there is hope for everyone.

Third, a reader must not introduce meanings into a work that are not really there. A proper Biblical perspective should be supplied by the reader or the discussion leader. But in setting up categories, as has been done here, there is always the danger of an artificial systematization, of forcing conclusions from the *observer's* viewpoint not intended by the author. What was the writer's purpose and intention? Can this work be experienced outside itself? Is the *critic* guilty of the heresy of paraphrase?

For example, some analysts, in examining this imaginative literature, have not been content to let the literary artist speak for him or herself.[35] In William Inge's *The Dark at the Top of the Stairs*, for example, some commentators saw portrayed the principles of Christian atonement and the presence of a Christ figure in the death of a young Jewish boy, when, or so it seems, the analogy was not originally intended by the author at all.

Sidney Lanier criticizes this type of interpretation in *Christianity and Crisis*, in an article titled "The Gospel According to Freud." In discussing *The Dark at the Top of the Stairs*, he not only points up the danger in audiences' "accepting unknowingly and uncritically the view of man offered in what purports to be a homely 'slice of life' "—ergo, a possible false prophetic voice; he also assails the philosophy implicit in the play, which he feels is "Latter-Day Freudianity." In such a Freudian homily fractured relationships are healed simply by accepting and recognizing the needs of others and by setting aright the male/female relationships between father and mother.

But even more significant—and this is the key concern—is the tendency of Christians to use such a play uncritically to illustrate the Gospel of Christ. Can there be Christian reconciliation without our blessed Lord Himself? Superimposing a definitely Christian redemption motif upon drama that should be viewed on its own grounds, Lanier holds, is "a dishonest kind of hitch-hiking and, like hitch-hiking, it is dangerous.[36]

Fuzzy thinking and its resultant implications present a dangerous threat to contemporary preachers. Today's homiletician who is struggling for *relevance* can become subtly trapped into these "questionable equations." In simple terms, it depends upon who's seeing the play. The Christian seeing Macleish's *J. B.* may read into it far different insights and values than the "good agnostic" who remarks to the spouse: "Darling, we must get that book." Lanier says in summary,

> It is all very well to point to *Dark at the Top of the Stairs* as an example of the reconciling power of God's love and the efficacy of forgiveness if you are speaking from within Christian experience. It is quite a different thing if you are speaking to the uncommitted, the seeking who now number a large proportion of our congregations. . . . There is no equivalent for the saving truth in Christ. It is dangerously misleading to marshal contemporary artists as witnesses to a God whom they do not yet acknowledge. We must take care that we do not unwittingly lead our flocks into an alien and sterile land.[37]

Christian Artisans

One further point needs to be mentioned. In alluding to the preacher's dilemma, Lanier comments on the preacher's reluctance to use Biblical illustrations exclusively because of the appalling Biblical illiteracy. But does Lanier press his point too far when he says that "unhappily, there is a marked dearth of compelling contemporary depictions of Christian experience in current plays, films, and novels"?

Admittedly, the bulk of writing that gluts the market is non-Christian. And much of purportedly Christian literature is titillating, mawkish, and flabby, as William Mueller has pointed out. But what of T. S. Eliot, Dorothy Sayers, Charles Williams, W. H. Auden, and Morris West,[38] not to mention the works of C. S. Lewis? Here indeed is rich lore in which to see the image of the Christ-man and the Christ-woman, which we shall consider in conclusion.

Christ-Man and Christ-Woman: The Biblical Portrait

What, then, shall we say? In much contemporary literature humanity by and of itself is stalemated because it has failed to solve its most basic problem, its estrangement from God—our Creator, Redeemer, and Sustainer. Everyone is a stranger to the person God intended in the creation and instead is degenerate as a result of the Fall into sin; but a wonderful potential is there for those who understand what, through Christ, is now possible. The types we have considered point to humanity's foremost need: life with and in God. To quote Mueller again,

> The serious student of modern fiction may discover that his reading eventuates in a self-knowledge alerting him to Biblical affirmations previously unnoticed. . . . The novelist will not save us, but he may well bring us to the knowledge that we are in need of salvation.[39]

Turning to the Gospels, we find the "true person," the "new person," in our blessed Lord and Savior. For he is at once the Person we are to be and the Power to become such a new creature.[40]

The apostle Paul spells out the process of cleaning the begrimed, painted-over canvas and letting the originally intended portrait begin to come through:

> This is my instruction, then, which I give you from God. Do not live any longer as the Gentiles live. For they live blindfolded in a world of illusion, and are cut off from the life of God through ignorance and insensitiveness. They have stifled their consciences and then surrendered themselves to sensuality, practicing any form of impurity which lust can suggest. But you have learned nothing like that from Christ, if you have really heard His voice and understood the truth that he has taught you. No, what you learned was to fling off the dirty clothes of the old way of living, which were rotted through and through with lust's illusion, and, with yourselves mentally and spiritually remade, to put on the clean fresh clothes of the new life which was made by God's design for righteousness—and the holiness which is no illusion.[41]

The Christ-man and the Christ-woman do not make the error of

1. *The person of complacency*, for he/she has become aware in the fullest, truest sense, of life's values—of what God has done in the person of his Son, Jesus Christ. One cannot be apathetic, for there is a new self inside, the Christ within. And one "cannot but speak of the things which he has seen and heard" (Acts 4:20).

The Christ-person does not make the error of

2. *The person of despair*, for one has a whole new life to rejoice in, now that one is living in God.

> Why art thou cast down, O my soul? And why art thou disquieted in me? Hope thou in God (Ps. 42:5)—If God be for us, who can be against us? (Rom. 8:31)—All things are yours (1 Cor. 3:21).

The Christ-person does not make the error of

3. *The person of defiance*, for one is overwhelmed by the love of the Father, a love so great, that "while we were yet sinners Christ died for us" (Rom. 5:8).

4. Nor can one be a *person of stubborn hope in self*; for having come face to face with the great God of redemption, God the Father, Son, and Holy Spirit, one can only say, "It is [God] that hath made us and not we ourselves" (Ps. 100:3) and can only affirm with Paul,

> He has delivered us from the dominion of darkness and transferred us to the kingdom of his beloved Son, in whom we have redemption, the forgiveness of sins . . . He is before all things, and in him all things hold together. He is the head of the body, the church; he is the Beginning, the first-born from the dead, that in everything he might be pre-eminent. For in him all the fullness of God was pleased to dwell, and through him to reconcile to himself all things, whether on earth or in heaven, making peace by the blood of his cross (Col. 1:13, 14, 17–20 RSV).
>
> O the depth of the riches both of the wisdom and knowledge of God! How unsearchable are his judgments, and his ways past finding out! For who hath known the mind of the Lord, or who hath been his counselor? Or who hath first given to him that it shall be recompensed to him again? For of him, and through him, and to him are all things, to whom be glory forever. Amen (Rom. 11:33–36).

This is the Christ-person, whose purpose in life is to glorify God . . . and to enjoy him forever. This is the image of humanity that we must bring to people everywhere, not forgetting the educated.

Perusing Pertinent Paperbacks

The following represents groups of literature up to the late seventies that were studied in the course "Reaching the Educated Adult." Many of the books are still in print or available in libraries. The reader may disagree with some of the classifications. The section is only illustrative. Although many cannot be recommended as Christian literature, some may serve to depict the human condition more clearly to us.

1. **Protean.** Tom Wolfe, *The Electric Kool-Aid Acid Test*; Nick Farina, *Been Down So Long It Looks Like Up to Me*; Erica Jong, *Fear of Flying*; works of Kurt Vonnegut, Jr.

2. **Complacency.** John Updike, *The Couples*; *Rabbit Redux*; John O'Hara, *The Hat on the Bed.*

3. **Despair.** James Joyce, *The Dead*; Franz Kafka, *The Trial*; *The Castle*; Eugene O'Neill, *Long Day's Journey into Night*; William Faulkner, *The Sound and the Fury*; Lawrence Durrell, *Justine*; John Steinbeck, *East of Eden.* Charles Webb, *The Graduate*; Evan Hunter, *Last Summer*; Ingmar Bergman's films, *The Seventh Seal*; *The Silence.*

4. **Defiance.** John Osborne, *Look Back in Anger*; James Jones, *From Here to Eternity*; Philip Wylie, *Opus 21*; *Generation of Vipers*; Jack Kerouac, *The Subterraneans*; *On the Road*; Joseph Heller, *Catch 22*; Ken Kesey, *One Flew over the Cuckoo's Nest*; Mario Puzo, *The Godfather*; Tennessee Williams (could also be classified as "neurotic-psychotic"), *Cat on a Hot Tin Roof*; *A Streetcar Named Desire*; Elia Kazan ("egomaniacal"), *The Arrangement*; J. D. Salinger (or "idealist"?), *Catcher in the Rye*; Sidney Sheldon, *The Other Side of Midnight.*

5. **Oppressed.** James Baldwin, *Another Country*; *The Fire Next Time*; *Go Tell It on the Mountain*; Ralph Ellison, *The Invisible Man*; Richard Wright, *Native Son.*

6. **Hedonist.** Henry Miller, *Tropic of Cancer*; *Tropic of Capricorn*; Pauline Reage, *The Story of O*; *Return to the Chateau*; Xaviera Hollander, *The Happy Hooker*; Lynda Jordan, *The Merry Madam*; Harold Robbins, *The Adventurers*; Robert H. Rimmer (or "utopian"?), *The Harrad Experiment.*

7. **Utopian.** Ayn Rand, *Anthem.*

8. **Nihilist.** (some might use the label "absurdite") Albert Camus, *Caligula*; *The Plague*; *The Stranger*; *The Fall*; Ernest Hemingway, *The Sun Also Rises*; *A Farewell to Arms*; Jean Paul Sartre, *No Exit.*

9. **Nothingness.** John Updike, *Rabbit, Run*; Albert Camus, *Cross Purposes*; Thomas Pynchon, *V*; Herman Hesse, *Demian; Siddhartha; Steppenwolf.*

10. **The "New Humanism."** Albert Camus, *The Myth of Sisy-*

phus. Cf. Nobel prize speeches of William Faulkner and Albert Camus.

11. **Objectivist.** Ayn Rand, *The Fountainhead*; *Atlas Shrugged.* Cf. *The Virtue of Selfishness*, ch. 11.

12. **Frustrated.** Alberto Moravia, *Conjugal Love*; *Ghost at Noon*; *The Fetish and Other Stories*; D. H. Lawrence, *Sons and Lovers*; *The Kangaroo*.

13. **Nostalgic.** Günter Grass, *The Tin Drum*; *Dog Years*; *Cat and Mouse*; F. Scott Fitzgerald, *The Great Gatsby*; George Lucas, *Gloria Katz & Willard Huyck*; *American Graffiti.*

14. **Political.** Ignazio Silone, *Bread and Wine*; *Fontamara.*

15. **Social Science Fiction.** Robert A. Heinlein, *Stranger in a Strange Land*; Ray Bradbury, *The Martian Chronicles*; Anthony Burgess, *Clockwork Orange*; Kurt Vonnegut, Jr., *Slaughter-House Five*; *Cat's Cradle*; *The Sirens of Titan.*

16. **"Hard" Science Fiction.** Isaac Asimov.

17. **Space Opera.** *Buck Rogers*; *Doc Savage.*

18. **Fantasy.** J. R. R. Tolkien, *The Lord of the Rings*; Erich von Däniken, *Chariots of the Gods*; *Gods from Outer Space*; Irving Wallace, *The Word*; Michael Crichton, *The Terminal Man*; Kurt Vonnegut, Jr., *God Bless You, Mr. Rosewater.*

19. **Psychotropic.** Carlos Castaneda, *The Teachings of Don Juan: A Yaqui Way of Knowledge*; *Journey to Ixtlan*; *The Lessons of Don Juan*; *A Separate Reality.*

20. **Enslaved**. Philip Roth, *Portnoy's Complaint*; Alexander Solzhenitsyn, *One Day in the Life of Ivan Denisovitch.*

21. **Failure.** Arthur Miller, *Death of a Salesman*; Saul Bellow, *Herzog*; William Golding, *The Spire*; D. H. Lawrence, *The Man Who Died*; Edward Albee, *Zoo Story*, *Sandbox*; *The American Dream*; *Who's Afraid of Virginia Woolf?* (or, with Herzog and T. S. Eliot's *The Cocktail Party*, more hope than despair?).

22. **Death-denying.** Robert Alley, *Last Tango in Paris.*

23. **The Christ-man/Christ-woman**. Leo Tolstoy, *The Death of Ivan Ilych*; Nathaniel Hawthorne, *The Scarlet Letter*; Herman Melville, *Billy Budd*; Fyodor Dostoevsky, *The Brothers Karamazov*; *Crime and Punishment*; *The Possessed*; *The Idiot*; T. S. Eliot, *Ash Wednesday*; *The Waste Land*; *Choruses from "The Rock"*; William Faulker, *A Fable*; *Intruder in the Dust*; *Light in August*; Graham Greene, *The Power and the Glory*; *The Heart of the Matter*; *A Burnt-*

Out Case; Richard Kim, *The Martyred*; Nikos Kazantzakis, *The Greek Passion*; *The Last Temptation of Christ*; Morris L. West, *The Devil's Advocate*; *The Shoes of the Fisherman*; *Second Victory*; Alan Paton, *Cry, The Beloved Country*; *Too Late the Phalarope*; John Updike, *Pigeon Feathers and Other Stories*; George Bernanos, *The Diary of a Country Priest.*

Secular Literature Today

Earlier reference was made to a pastor in San Diego who was a member of a literary society which did not discuss an author's work until the writer had been dead for five years. The current popularity of a novel, play, or TV program does not mean it will have lasting significance. Many of the works previously cited continue to have literary value. But it is intriguing to assess the passing scene of literature and muse about which stars will rise briefly and fall, and which will continue to glow as they bear the repeated probing of literary critics and English lit majors.

Granted, many people are not reading worthwhile literature today. The "tube" has taken over. And those "educated" on a university campus are also often not reading novels, much less the classics. But *great* literature still remains a vital resource for the Christian apologist as the "prophetic voices in modern fiction" reveal the handwriting on the wall, showing us where our culture is heading. While this assessment is being made, new insights into personal nature can be made as the images evoked by the writing mirror one's own self.

Most of all, one discovers a common ground of interest shared by the apologist and the "educated" where dialog can begin—and, perhaps ultimately, the presentation of the *Good News* of Jesus and the resurrection (Acts 8:35).

As one student put it in the Spring 1988 session of Reaching the Educated Adult,

Course Review

When I walked into your classroom on that first day of class, I was expecting a curriculum in which I would learn how to teach the Christian Adult or Educated Adult, using religious materials already on the market or by writing my own.

> But I was delightfully surprised to find that that was not what the course was about at all. For what I learned from this course is that, in order to reach the educated adult, one must know where the educated adult is in life. Or another way of putting it is, one must know what questions the educated adult is asking and where he is getting those questions.
>
> And the only way to find those questions is to get away from the theological books of the seminary (not that they are unimportant) and get into the literature of today. I've discovered through this course that if I really care about reaching the educated adults for Christ I must find a common ground in which I can meet them and challenge them with the Gospel. Since the educated adult reads, so must I.
>
> I also discovered that I can reach others by listening to their music, seeing their movies, watching their television programs and reading their newspapers and periodicals. It is only by taking the time to meet them on their ground that I can have any hope of bringing them the Gospel of Jesus Christ.
>
> My favorite quote from *The Compassionate Mind* is one taken from Luther: "Without knowledge of literature pure theology cannot at all endure." If I learned anything this quarter, one thing I learned well: I must constantly be reading, not only theological books, but secular books as well, for it is in those books that the educated adult acquires his philosophy of life. It is my hope that that philosophy will be one that is in harmony with the Gospel of Jesus Christ, and if not, my challenge is to bring it into such harmony.

Whom might we single out on the literary horizon today? Only a few representative authors will be noted. John Updike is immediately recognized as a leading writer of our generation. He also knows Christian theology. One of his most powerful poems is about the resurrection. He has written articles on Barth, Brunner, and Tillich. In the sixties in response to a letter from a student of mine doing a study on him for our course. Updike wrote,

> I was raised as a Lutheran in Pennsylvania—if you had read my writing, notably the story *Pigeon Feathers* and one account of my boyhood in *Five Boyhoods* (Doubleday), you would know this. My wife is the daughter of a Unitarian minister. We are all now Congregationalists and our children are being raised as such.
>
> Sincerely,
> John Updike

Granted, Updike's background may not qualify him as a Biblical theologian, but knowing his background and building on the opinions he expresses, we have a natural opportunity to discuss basic Christian doctrine with the reader.

I believe Updike's work *Rabbit, Run* was his greatest literary achievement. He has not since equaled the power of description in that masterwork. Important for our purposes is that he grapples with basic ontological questions—what it means to *be*, to *exist*. Guilt is hardly Rabbit's problem. Note the funeral scene after the death of his child, accidently drowned by his wife in a bathtub. Rabbit mirrors many modern persons who feel less guilt than wonder about the very purpose of existence. This is a major issue for the apologist who in dialog often must deal with questions of the First Article of the Apostles' Creed (creation) before those of the Second Article (redemption).

I am of the opinion that Updike's *The Couples* was far more than a sex farce. Like William Golding's *The Lord of the Flies*, it was a disquisition on original sin.

But the last twenty years of Updike's work have been disappointing to me. *Trust Me*, his latest collection of short stories, again demonstrates his gifts as a writer with brilliant insights into the human condition. However, it is a giant step from there to portray the human being as a redeemed Christian struggling in the real world. This is the Biblical corrective that must always be supplied.

Andrew Greeley, priest-turned-novelist, gave us some powerful passages in some of his earliest fiction. There was the death scene of a thirteen-year-old girl, with a prayer by a priest that moved me to tears. The girl had been struck by a hit-and-run driver. She told the priest at her bedside,

> "Kevin," said the dying girl. "Are you here, Kevin?"
> "Yes, Patsy, I'm here." It did not sound like my voice at all.
> "May I hold your hand until Jesus takes it? He's my real father."
> Mike signaled me that it was only a matter of moments.
> The young priest handed me the ritual.
> "In the name of God the almighty Father who created you,
> In the name of Jesus Christ, Son of the living God,
> who suffered for you,
> In the name of the Holy Spirit who was poured out upon you,
> Go forth, faithful Christian.

May you live in peace this day,
may your home be with God in Zion,
with Mary the Virgin Mother of God,
with Joseph, and all the angels and saints.
"My sister in faith,
I entrust you to God who created you.
May you return to the one
who formed you from the dust of this earth.
May Mary, the angels, and all the saints
come to meet you as you go forth from this life.
May Christ who was crucified for you
bring you freedom and peace.
May Christ, the Son of God, who died for you
take you into his Kingdom.
May Christ, the Good Shepherd,
give you a place within his flock.
May he forgive your sins
and keep you among his people.
May you see your Redeemer face to face
and enjoy the sight of God forever."

> Just as I finished the prayer, Patsy extended her arms as though she were embracing someone. "Oh, yes, I'm ready now," she said in a voice that was filled with sweetness and love.
>
> Then she died.[42]

There was the stirring, final collapse of Ellen. She finally admits her hatred of God and the church and makes her confession, and the priest responds,

> "And now you have done it," I said, feeling a huge burden lift away and go spiraling off into space. "And the damn-fool Church says, 'Ellen Foley Curran Strauss, we really didn't notice you were gone, because we never let you go.' "
>
> She put her head against my knee and wept. Then she gathered herself together and said, "So Ellen's worst sin was against Ellen... For these and all the sins of my life I am heartily sorry and ask pardon of God and penance and absolution of you, Father."[43]

But in my opinion Greeley's novels have progressively deteriorated. They have certainly been "successful" if it is true that in the first month after publication of one of his books 1,135,000 copies were sold. Or is it that Catholics and others love reading explicit lip-tonguing depictions of the sex lives of priests and nuns?[44] Greeley has seriously attempted to make statistical analyses of Roman Catholics' reactions to his novels, to determine whether, after reading them, they understand better the relationship between religion and sex and have "a more gracious image of God."[45] He has also written *Confessions of a Parish Priest*[46] in which he spells out the rationale for the type of writing that he does. But is that the only type of writing he will do in the future?

Danielle Steel has over 100 million copies of her books in print. *The San Francisco Chronicle* reported that she told a San Francisco literary society that more copies of her books were in print than of all the authors present combined. We must take her impact on our culture seriously. At this writing Danielle Steel is the most widely read writer by University of California-Berkeley women students. But it is generic pap, the work of a photographer. It holds up a camera to life and merely mirrors it. It does not wrestle with the great ontological questions of life as does Camus. It is not literature.

Also at the top of the shelf at the airport book stalls are Jean Auel, Saul Bellow, Thomas Pinchon, Philip Roth, J. R. R. Tolkien, Stephen King, Robert Ludlum, James Mitchener, Anne Tyler, Mary Higgins Clark, Jeffrey Archer, Sidney Sheldon, Barbara Taylor Bradford, Scott Turow, Ken Follett—fill in your own favorites. Serious readers are also absorbed in the works of writers outside the United States such as V. S. Naipaul, Gabriel Garcia Marquez, Nadine Gordimer, and Iris Murdock.

Add to this the science fiction, mysteries, historical romances, and westerns (especially Louis L'Amour), and you have a brief picture of America's current books reading habits.

A helpful study could assess how and why America's (especially university students') reading interests have changed in the last generation.

But more important, Where are the Christian writers? Where are the Dostoevskis of *our* age? Why are there not more Morris Wests and Frederick Buechners in whose writing we might see the Christ-man and the Christ-woman, also struggling, "drawn and quartered in the rushing wheel of the modern world"—yet as *Christ's* men and women?

The task of the literary artist is not to practice theology. Otto Piper presumably once said that a novelist or a writer is not a theologian, and a theologian is not a writer. The task of the Christian literary artist (were more of them to appear) is not to produce sermons disguised as literature, though one does hope to see more Christian fiction in the marketplace. (But just try to get "clean" Christian fiction published!)

The paucity of authentic Christian characters and Christian experience in current fiction leads to several observations.

By *authentic Christian characters* I do *not* mean a clean, proper, outwardly pious individual. A person who *looks* Christian might not be. Authentic Christian characters are *simul justus et peccator*—at one and the same time justified before God because of their faith in the redemption by Jesus Christ, yet sinners because their original sinful nature keeps breaking through. A perfect, righteous type does not exist and is not a true character.

I believe that Keith Miller's books some years ago sold in the millions of copies because he recognized not only the redeemed Christian's potential for greatness but also his inherent tendency for destructiveness and sin (*A Taste of New Wine, A Second Touch, Habitation of Dragons, The Becomers*, etc.). He did not depict a stereotyped, blond, blue-eyed, Bible-under-arm ("God-in-a-box") Christian, striding off to church, all problems solved. He portrayed a Christian of clay feet with chinks in the armor. *Vulnerability* was the prevailing tone. It was Paul's "Not that I have already obtained all this . . . but I press on . . . " (Phil. 3:12 NIV). *That* Christian was credible.

A classic case of *simul justus et peccator* is seen in the whiskey priest in Graham Greene's *The Power and the Glory*. The priest is a drunk, a lecher, a coward, fleeing from the law. But Greene with "creative literary artistry" still reveals him clinging by his fingernails to the grace of God. And the crowning touch, as R. W. B. Lewis says in *The Picaresque Saint*,

> The entire pattern is nevertheless artistically redeemed by a full awareness of the grotesque disproportion between the model and its reenactment.
>
> The priest is about to be executed. . . . The priest giggled; he couldn't stop himself. He said, "I don't think martyrs are like this."
>
> It is the giggle that saves both the priest and the novel Greene has written about him. For it is when he laughs that we know this slovenly rogue, this unshaven *picaro*, to be also a saint; and we

> know that here for once—as in only one or two other novels—the paradoxes have held firm and the immense delicate balance has been maintained.[47]

Where are the Christian writers, respected by the literary world as artists and yet true to their Christian faith in their writing? But given that dearth, why doesn't the Christian apologist make more use of the existing literature—such as it is—for dialog about the Christian faith? Missionaries in the Orient use Steinbeck and Faulkner (the lure of America) to dialog with university students. They read the work together, then ask the question, But is *this* the meaning and purpose of life?

I recall a Stanford student, an agnostic, who with puzzlement picked up his Christian friend's copy of Camus's *The Fall*. "Why are *you* reading *this*, Lloyd?" he asked. Fruitful dialog ensued.

The theological insights in secular literature are also boundless for Christians wanting to plumb more deeply how to live out the Christian faith in contemporary society. For those wavering in the faith, fiction can be a profound aid in grappling with Christian truth where a theological textbook may fail. Amos Wilder has said that in one's effort at self-understanding cultural images and works of art are needed. Literature assists in the search for self-understanding. "Philosophy and theology as rational disciplines are inadequate to the process."

I remember a professional church worker at the University of California in Berkeley who had lost her faith completely but returned to it upon reading the poetry of T. S. Eliot. Our very familiarity with Scripture can sometimes dull our Christian senses (with the Enemy's help), whereas great secular literature can alert us to Biblical affirmations previously unnoticed.

The novelist will not save us, but he may well bring us to the knowledge that we are in need of salvation.[48]

Therein lies a clue. The purpose of literature may not be so much to show us what the Christian faith and lifestyle *is*, but what it *is not*. And then we are driven back to the Gospels again, God's inspired Word, where alone we meet the kind of person we are to be, and the power to become that *new creation*—a *little Christ*.

Meanwhile literature can give us that sharpened view from the sycamore tree. The following letter is a case in point. It is an *un-*

solicited response received when I was contacting students for permission to quote their material in a sourcebook of readings on this theme. The former student is now an associate pastor in a middle-sized California parish with a well-educated, mostly older membership.

> When I took the class Reaching the Educated Adult, I truly enjoyed it, and profited from it. But I must admit, I was somewhat dismayed by the characterization of the bulk of non-churched, educated people in some pretty negative terms, defiant, hedonist, despairing, nihilist, protean, and all the others. My fairly sheltered experience hadn't given that impression.
>
> After several years in the parish, I have found that your characterizations are more accurate than I wanted to admit. There is a great deal of despair out there, leading to most of those other philosophies of life. The most common place where I have encountered such people is in nonchurched family members (such as husbands or adult children) of active members. Some of the understandings and approaches which we dealt with in your class have been most helpful.
>
> I also value the way in which you took the issue of humanism as a contact point with which to introduce people to Christ. Much of the fundamentalist (and well-publicized) reaction to "the evils of secular humanism" are causing more distrust of the church than they are helping.

The above comment is a perfect setting for the following discussion. Rather than attacking humanism broadside for its self-centeredness and anti-God arrogance, humanism can also be seen as a contact point for dialog and a bridge for pointing the educated to the *source* of the good in humanity—our Lord Himself.[49] It is in that spirit that I have written the following brief essays, *Descending to Transcend, The Pizzeria,* and *The Long, Dark Tunnel.*

Descending to Transcend: The Compassionate Mind of Albert Camus

"People aren't looking for a 'just God' any more," said my colleague over lunch at the pizzeria. "Nor are they seeking to 'be justified' before God. Their number one concern is *their job*. When that goes, they lose their security, their home, their life-style, the American Dream."

Layoffs hit the educated as well as the blue-collar worker. A thirty-eight-year-old Yuppie in San Mateo with a Ph.D. in electrical engineering puts a plastic bag over his head and leaves behind his wife and three children. He was over-qualified and had been without work for months. An executive's Taurus station wagon in the neighborhood vanishes and a beat up VW wagon takes its place. Another pink slip. Stress kits are the order of the day. And one wonders how many of the obituaries in the *San Francisco Chronicle* are linked to the "early retirement" announced not long before.

But what is the worldview of the educated *while* the job is not threatened and *before* the bubble has burst? As we have seen, the literary artist can give us some insightful clues. For several reasons I turn particularly to Albert Camus for more extended consideration. For one, he raises Biblical/theological questions in a profound and arresting way. I remember a seminary student who appeared at my office with bloodshot eyes early one morning. He had spent most of the night reading Camus's *The Fall*, which I believe is one of the greatest novels in the last generation. "I haven't had such a horrible look at myself in a long time!" he groaned. Somehow the Book of Romans had not been doing that for him. *The Fall* did. He was *overfamiliar* with the Scriptures. But he had seen great Biblical truths in the writings of a non-Christian author.

Finally, I have selected Camus because I have found that much of his personal philosophy typifies the thinking of many of the educated I have known. As a campus pastor and graduate student at the University of California-Berkeley in the fifties until now I find many of my non-Christian friends espouse Camus's vision of the world. It is a complex view that entails secularity, non-conformity, autonomy, absurdity, indifference, and the impossibility of redemption. And yet at times it also enigmatically comprises a vision of the possible, an atheological hope in man and a compassionate mind which expresses itself in a life of self-giving service to others. Similar threads of thought are woven through the tapestry of Camus's own life and that of the characters in his works.

Albert Camus was born in Mondovi, Algeria, in 1913, the son of Spanish and French parents. He had a happy childhood and grew up in Algeria. He earned a degree in philosophy and after several jobs tried journalism.

In the thirties he joined a theatrical company, and during World War II was active in the French Resistance, editing the important underground paper *Combat*. In occupied France in 1942, at the age of 29, he published *The Myth of Sisyphus* and *The Stranger*. Among his major writings are *The Rebel, The Plague, The Fall, Exile and the Kingdom*, and *Caligula and Three Other Plays.* He was awarded the Nobel Prize for Literature in 1957.

R. W. B. Lewis observes that Camus's thought contains baffling inconsistencies, indeed contradictions. *The Rebel*, he feels, is nothing other than St. Augustine's *City of God* written backwards.[50] What follows, accordingly, is my stream-of-consciousness attempt at probing what Lewis calls his "flat and reckless formulas the reverse of which may often be quite equally true."[51]

Camus's starting point is *indifference*. Indeed, his character Sisyphus mirrors the bland indifference of the universe. Although he is faced with meaningless, ceaseless toil, pushing a boulder up the mountainside until it slips out of his grasp and he must repeat the climb, Camus says we must conclude that Sisyphus is happy. He leaves him at the foot of the mountain. He has no need for a disgruntled God who came into the world and prefers futile sufferings on a cross. *Descender plus bas pour monter plus hautement* (Descend still lower to climb still higher.)

Camus plumbs "the depths of our nihilism . . . search[ing] only for reasons to transcend it."[52] His aim is positive and always intellectual. And since Camus ultimately goes beyond indifference to hope in man, Lewis feels he stands for the compassionate mind.

He is compassionate because he is interested in humanity and the very reason for existence in a senseless universe from which God has withdrawn. "Men die and they are not happy" (*Caligula*).

It is *absurdus* (harsh, grating), *surdus* (deaf), a timeless universe, tone-deaf that Camus refuses to accept (as Kierkegaard and Kafka do) with a "blind leap of faith beyond the limits of scandalized reason."[53] Rather he affirms the dignity of man, the tragedy of human dignity. And his secular faith affirms that man will "rediscover at last the wine of the absurd and the bread of indifference out of which his greatness will be nourished."[54]

We are *The Stranger*. Ours is the religion of the exalted present.

It is a life surrounded by death beyond which there is an enormity of nothing. The absence of a future and the flat dismissal of illusory hope lead us to "count on nothing and to consider the present as the only truth which is given us."[55]

> The only sin . . . is a blindness to the beauty of this life in the foolish hope of another.[56]

There is the intolerable penalty of man not only being born to die; he is condemned to die. And yet he is happy in the face of it all and opens his heart to the tender indifference of the world. Ergo, we have the absurd man, whose indifference matches the indifference of the universe.[57]

In this enigmatic world, one is convicted more for indifference than for a crime (like Meursault in *The Stranger*). But, as Lewis notes, Camus denies that his fiction is to any dependable extent autobiographical. For he personally confronts death "as the only way of getting at an honest and even a positive estimate of life."[58] What then began as the only true philosophical problem—suicide—Camus rejects and transforms it into "the vision of the possible." It is a man who is not absurd at all who chooses time and history, against God and the eternal. Committed to human reason, he decries those who, faced with absurdity, do not say "Absurd!" but say "God!"[59] He does not acquiesce and throw himself into God's arms with "the leap" (quoting Nietzsche in *Thus Spake Zarathustra*), "one fatal leap, a poor ignorant weariness that does not want to want any more: this created all gods and afterworlds."

But—and here is the Achilles' heel—have not Nietzsche and Camus and many of the educated today also created the god they reject? Camus's "fragment of Christianity" is of an "extreme, an unmodulated other-worldliness (or after-worldliness)"[60] that is not the true, full nature of Christianity at all.

Thus, without the revealed vision of God in Christ, one hears only allusions to the language of Christianity and the New Testament.

> In *Cross-Purposes*, the mocking faint remainders of the New Testament serve only to intensify the anguish and despair of the final revelation—the total impossibility of divine intervention.[61]

One wonders how many of the educated today are touched more by his final humanistic hope (which we will soon see) rather than by the hope*lessness* of some of his protagonists—the pitiless "No!" in *Cross-Purposes* or the "Nothing!" in *Caligula*.

I sat in the front row of a small theatre near Fisherman's Wharf in San Francisco during the Beatnik era and saw *Caligula* performed. I heard Caligula's sadistic, nihilistic prayer:

> Instruct us in the truth of this world which is not to have any truth.... Overwhelm us with thy gifts, spread across our faces thy impartial cruelty, thy objective hatred; open before our eyes thy hands full of flowers and of murders.... Give us thy passions without object, thy griefs deprived of reason, thy joys without future.... Any thou, so empty and so burning, inhuman and yet so earthly, make us drunk with the wine of thy equivalence and press us forever to thy dark and mordant heart.[62]

I heard Cherea say,

> To lose one's life is a little thing, and I will have the courage when necessary. But to see the sense of this life dissipated, to see our reason for existence disappear: that is what is insupportable. A man cannot live without reason.[63]

I still vividly remember, after thirty years, the bloodied, mortally wounded Caligula confront us in the last scene with defiant absurdity, crying, "I am still alive!"

I wondered, as I do now, how many theatre-goers stepped out into the foggy air of Baghdad by the Bay and went back to the wine of the absurd and the bread of indifference—and how many went home with *a compassionate mind*. For that is what Camus moved toward in his own version. It was not a compassion that came from God, however.

> For by the late 1940s Camus had inched his way to and had settled upon his own truncated precept of charity—leaving the Lord to take care of Himself, and being content with loving one's neighbor.[64]

His was a secular redemption which had moved from solitude, nihilism, and absurdity to a sense of participation in society. Lewis says the first article of Camus's slender humanistic creed thus became compassion. But I would add, it was not the compassion that comes from Christ but from within one's own self. "It is the *suffering* of mankind that seized the mind and imagination of Camus; and so it is the suffering that he enjoins us to share."[65]

Camus says he is tired of "criticism, denigration, and meanness—in short, of nihilism." He says he will never abandon the hope. And as R. W. B. Lewis concludes, "Camus has been faithful to his own vision, and he has a rock to build upon."[66]

But that rock was not Christ.

The spirit of Camus is very much alive today. Many of the educated whom I have known would swear by his creed,"If we consent to do without God and without hope, we are not resigned to do without man."[67]

Others might reflect Sisyphus, or Cherea, or Meursault. Some are like Jean Baptiste Clamence in *The Fall*, who while admitting *mea culpa*, subtly shifted his guilt to *nostra culpa* ("the state of us all!"), and went on to become a "judge-penitent" of others, for whom the idea of redemption was inconceivable—"Fortunately!"

But another Prodigal Son, in the gospels, came to a different conclusion. He came to the realization that there *was* hope—*outside* himself. And he "came to his senses" and went back to a forgiving, compassionate Waiting Father.[68]

This God was known by Tobina Dalton, a woman who studied with me a few years ago. She was a person of deep intellect and singular resourcefulness. It usually took her four hours to get to class from her home, using four different modes of transportation. In correspondence with me after taking the course Reaching the Educated Adult she described her experiences in making door-to-door calls for her church in Stockton, California:

> I am reminded of that English Bishop who once said, "Everywhere St. Paul went there was a revolution, but everywhere I go they serve tea!"
>
> It was not exactly tea that I was served. I found carefully locked and bolted doors, intricate fences and neatly enameled signs like, "The owner of this house is armed"—and he had his dog tied to the doorknob!; or, "Ring door bell only in emergency, grouchy old man;" or, "We are happy the way we are. Thank you for not bothering me with your religion."
>
> I have had doors slammed in my face, but I also had the ones who said, "You made my day." One young fellow blurted out, "My old lady just left me; come and see what she gave up." Or a widow in her early sixties, "Does your church have ballroom dancing?"

> The world I find behind these doors is not impressed by the Bible or by the church or by preaching. But it is a needy world that needs to be confronted with God's love. I am reminded of Albert Camus: in his novel *The Stranger,* where he delicately paints a memorable picture of a human being caught and helpless in the grip of life, like a lethargic fly in the web of a predatory spider.[69]

It was Albert Camus that Tobina Dalton focused on in her study project. After her presentation to the class she spread a tablecloth on the desk, set out her china which she had brought, and provided us with tea and cookies. And then we discussed her memorable presentation.

It was actually a combined study of "The Netherlands at War" and "Glimpses into the Thought of Albert Camus." Tobina Dalton had worked in the Resistance, as had Camus, but her response to the war years was markedly different from his.

She said she had encountered a combination of the person of nihilism, nothingness, defiance, complacency, the political person, the enslaved person, and the person of the new humanism. But she also knew the possible person, who was born in utmost extremity, who became that new creation of which the Apostle Paul speaks.

> During 1940–45 we were literally driven back to the Old Testament stories and the gospels. In the face of death and execution, we discovered who we are and whose we are, whence we came and where we are going, and there we met Him, who is the person we are to become and the power to be that new creation: our Lord Himself.[70]

As she compared those thoughts with Camus's writings, she began to feel a strange empathy for this man who rose above nihilism to faith in humanity. It was only superficially that his seemed a philosophy of pessimism and despair. Rather it was much more a creed "which calls on men and women for the most heroic kind of affirmation of life."[71]

From the Biblical viewpoint—a perspective one cannot expect from a secular writer—the fact that everyone is our brother and sister requires a realization of the fatherhood of God; and that in turn can be known only because of Jesus Christ revealed in Scripture.

Tobina Dalton, who understands this, probed the characters of Camus with brilliant, incisive analysis, correlating them with the Resistance leaders she had known in Holland. Then she concluded with a compassionate challenge:

How do we answer the Camuses and Rieuxes[72] *in life? Did Christ solve the problems of rebellion, evil and death on Golgotha?*

Tobina Dalton's answer is that

> Camus (Rieux, and others) saw Christ too much in terms of traditional passion mysticism and too little as the protesting God involved in human sorrow and suffering, much less as the God of atonement and reconciliation and the swallowing up of death. Yes, Camus did see that Christ's cross must mean that God himself experienced the agony of death, but he could not see the deathly anguish of the godforsakenness in God. He saw God vanish on the cross, but he did not see Christ's death on the cross taken up into God. Camus has to understand God's being in the godforsakenness of Christ. Only when he recognizes what took place between Jesus and his Father on the cross, and then only, can he speak of the significance of this God for those who suffer and protest at the history of the world. The only way past protest-atheism is through a theology of the cross that understands God as the suffering God in the suffering of Christ and that cries out with the godforsaken God, "My God, why have you forsaken me?" Then God's being is in suffering and the suffering is in God's being itself, because God is love. It takes the metaphysical rebellion up into itself, because it recognizes in the cross of Christ a rebellion in metaphysics or better a rebellion in God himself. God himself loves and suffers the death of Christ in his love. He is no cold, heavenly power, nor does he tread his way over the corpses of Dachau, Mauthausen, and Vietnam, but is known as the human God in the crucified son of man.
>
> We see this all through the Old Testament and especially in the history of Israel, in the exodus and in the exile. God already renounces his honor in the beginning at creation. Like a servant he carries the torch before Israel into the wilderness. Like a servant he bears Israel and its sins on his back. He descends into the thornbush, the Ark of the covenant and the temple.[73]
>
> His lamentation and sorrow over Israel in the exile show that God's whole existence with Israel is in suffering. Israel is the apple of his eye. He cannot forget Israel's suffering. He goes with Israel into the Babylonian exile. In his indwelling in the people he suffers

> with the people, goes with them into prison, feels sorrow with the martyrs. So conversely, the liberation of Israel also means the liberation of that "indwelling God" from its suffering. God himself was led out with Israel from Egypt. The redemption is for me and for you. The suffering of God is not futile; for it is the means by which Israel is redeemed. God himself is the ransom for Israel.

Read *Night*, a book written by E. Wiesel, a survivor of Auschwitz who so shatteringly and poignantly writes about how the SS hanged two men and a youth in front of the whole camp. The men died quickly, but the death throes of the youth lasted for half an hour.

> "Where is God? Where is he?" someone behind me asked.... Then the march past began.... And we had to look him full in the face. He was still alive when I passed in front of him. His tongue was still red, his eyes were not yet glazed.
>
> Behind me, I heard the same man asking, "Where is God now?" And I heard a voice within me answer him, "Where is he? Here he is—He is hanging here on this gallows."[74]

Caution is in order here. Wiesel's dialog can be properly understood, not as a form of passion mysticism, but as evidence that, regardless of how much this young man suffered, Christ had suffered *for* him so that this young man ultimately could triumph. There cannot be any other Christian answer to the question of this torment and the myriads of other torments. When God became man in Jesus of Nazareth, he not only entered into the finitude of man, but in his suffering on the cross entered into our godforsakenness, so that all the godless and the godforsaken can experience communication with him. There is no loneliness, no rejection, no pain, no torture which he has not taken to himself and assumed for us on the cross. As Paul says in Romans 6:8, the believer really participates in the suffering of God in the world. Man is summoned to share in God's sufferings at the hands of a godless world. It is not the religious act that makes the Christian, but as a Christian he participates in the sufferings of God in the secular life.

* * * * * * * * * * * *

Camus, you are mistaken when you say 1) that Christianity often keeps man from total involvement in his time and from feeling the agony of the human experiment, 2) or that Christianity creates a climate of indifference to human suffering, but you are so close when you say, *Descender plus bas pour monter plus hautement!*

Camus's difficulties with Christianity are not an easy task to unravel. His indictment shifts and changes, filled with sympathy for what Christianity is and tries to be, but he regrets deeply a number of attitudes Christianity instills, especially in *The Plague* which he calls "more anti-Christian than my earlier books." Why? Because it reflects a conviction about the division and incompatibility between the religious impulse and human sympathy and, of course, Camus sides with the latter. Only by saying No to the official pieties of the age could Camus sustain and enlarge that compassion he had come to believe in as the "redeemed" condition of man.[75]

* * * * * * * * * * * *

Many of the educated of today, autonomous and nonconformist as they are, incarnate a "new humanism" of secularity which is mirrored in the person—and in some of the characters—of Albert Camus. But how close they could be to the Kingdom of God! If only they could recognize the One who descended still lower to climb still higher—for us.

Who was it who said that if Albert Camus had lived longer in his search (which R. W. B. Lewis says for him *was* for the truth),[76] he would either have had to commit suicide or become a Catholic? Maybe he might have met "the God he never knew" (quite unlike the god he had declared dead)[77] who *did* descend in the person of his Son—to earth and even to death—that we might ascend still higher with him in the resurrection.

Tobina Dalton has pointed to the key for our witness to the Camuses of the world—and the Ingmar Bergmans—who repeat the question "How can a loving God let the innocent suffer?" Our response lies in directing them to *the godforsakenness in God.*

That is what Camus missed seeing at the cross—Christ's death taken up into God. God's being must be understood in the godforsakenness of Christ. Only then can Camus speak of the significance of God for those who suffer.

Our response to the Camuses and Bergmans of the world is to point them to a properly understood *theology of the cross.*[78] God suffers in the suffering Christ and cries out with the godforsaken

God, "My God, why have you forsaken me?" As Dalton says, "Then God's being is in suffering and the suffering is in God's being itself, because God is love."

So God in Christ's death entered into our godforsakenness so all the godless and godforsaken can have reconciliation with him. *No one*—the boy hung in *Night*, or the boy dying in *The Plague*, or the blonde girl raped and murdered in *Virgin Spring*—*no one* has loneliness, rejection, pain or torture which God himself has not absorbed in the cross of his Son.

When non-Christians lay aside their diminutive conception of God and deal with the godforsakenness in God (with Christ), they will have confronted the *true* God.

And then they must see this God alive in *us*.

What is needed is that we live out our lives of commitment to Christ—who alone is the source of compassion—in the world in which the educated live.

One setting in which this takes place is *The Pizzeria*.

The Pizzeria and *The Long Dark Tunnel* which follow were written by the author to illustrate how theological concepts may be applied in writing literature. Christian writers can integrate Biblical understandings as they write. Christian teachers can find opportunities to inject theological insights and applications when discussing writing that does not clearly reflect Biblical understandings or may even be written to reject the Christian view.

The Pizzeria

An Elderly Professor Overhears Some Students' Theological Dialog

Dr. Karl Altenbrenner, retired philosophy professor, University of California-Berkeley, basked in the warm sun that streamed through the restaurant window. He listened to the Campanile bells chime the noon hour as an increasing number of students crowded into the pizzeria, a half block off campus. It was just like the old days.

He heard the raucous conversation of some Cal students with—he assumed—friends from the nearby Graduate Theological Union. Already they were heatedly into their usually intense, but amiable, conversation. When an acquaintance joined the group, one student said,

"So you're one of those theological students in the God-business? Well, let me tell you what my sister said to the hospital chaplain on her deathbed as she was dying of cancer, 'Damn God! It only took Jesus several hours to die on the cross. I've been suffering for *twenty-six years!* My *doctor* has been the only one to relieve my pain—a little. God hasn't lifted His little finger to help me. Damn God!' "

Karl recalled that he had felt that way at one time. How clever he had been about it. Three hundred students, mostly the fraternity and sorority crowd, packed his witty philosophy lectures in Dwinelle Hall on the Cal campus. A classic, genial skeptic, he would masterfully defend a philosopher's position the first half hour then demolish his ideas the second. He would close the session with a cynical wag of the head and a raised eyebrow, intimating the utter futility of it all. Then he would leave them with his classic challenge, Is the question, *Is there meaning and purpose in life?* a *relevant* question?

Students clapped resoundingly. Then he would strut out of the classroom and over to the pizzeria where he held court with the students at a favorite table near the front window. He called it his "office."

Karl's thoughts shifted as he sat there alone. He stopped reminiscing when his attention was drawn to a grubbily-dressed campus expatriate, obviously on drugs, standing at the door of the restaurant, snapping his fingers towards the ground every few minutes while chanting incoherently to an invisible audience.

Then there was "The Dude," as they dubbed him, who rolled in on his motorbike dressed in a different outfit each day. He would set himself up at a table with a rose in a vase and a chilled bottle of champagne, grooving to the rock music coming through his earphones.

Karl remembered the time he had held a colleague's arm on a slick, rainy street. A 19-year-old coed had looked at the two of them with a faint, knowing smile. Across the street the Moonies usually set up their chart and started their lectures on *The Divine Principle*. That was Berkeley in the seventies.

Each day resembled a fast-moving movie screen. A paraplegic

in an electric wheelchair. A beautiful black-haired girl racing her bike down Euclid Avenue, at high noon, pigtails flying, as she headed back to school after an early lunch. She got her Ph.D. in Econ and went on to teach at Harvard.

He recalled the time an epileptic had had a fit right behind his chair. He had been sitting quietly nearby for 45 minutes. Karl quickly pushed his wallet in the man's mouth (he was chewing his tongue bloody) and asked if anyone knew anything about seizures. But everyone pretended they hadn't noticed. They just picked up their trays silently and moved to the back of the room.

Eric Hoffer, Joanna Dewey (John Dewey's granddaughter), Mario Savio—they all had been there. On St. Patrick's Day the owners served pitchers of green beer. Of course the chile tasted green, too, some days. One day someone had called the fire department because his old Buick convertible was leaking gas down the gutter. He had just gotten in and started up the car, and as he drove away one fireman had said, "Is he really going to *drive* that thing!"

He had often seen elderly persons in their seventies and eighties walk by. They walked and walked. No place to go. No one to talk to! Walk! Walk! One man touched each tree as he passed. Another stepped on every crack in the pavement.

High school kids soared by on their skateboards. And the college students (younger every year!) hurried to class. They had their whole lives ahead of them! On their faces he could see expectation, confidence, resoluteness.

The loud conversation nearby pulled him back to the present. With about a dozen students from the university and the seminaries at one table, he heard only bits and pieces of varied conversations.

"And so for nine years I prayed to God to give me faith. I read my Bible every night. But he never gave it to me."

"But did you ever ask God for forgiveness . . . ?"

"Well, if all the philosophers and great minds of history can't answer such questions, how can I?"

"You're still begging the question. You and I still have to cope with all the evil in the world—and in ourselves."

"I like one of the graffiti in the men's room here: 'Life is the interruption of an otherwise peaceful non-existence.' "

"I still agree with Dr. Rieux in Albert Camus's *The Plague*. Remember? After the child dies in agony, he says he refuses to accept a scheme of things in which children are put to torture. And all the priest says is that perhaps we should love what we cannot understand. Then Dr. Rieux says that since the world is shaped by death it might be better for God if we refused to believe in him—that we should struggle with all our might against death 'without raising our eyes toward the heaven where he sits in silence.' "

"Hey, Hal, I know. I have no easy theological answer for you. But, you know, I heard about a pastor in the East who preached the first of two Easter morning sermons. After the first service, a family went home, and their 9-year-old boy fell off the top of a bunk bed, suffered a blow to his temple, and died instantly. The parents called the pastor. The father greeted him at the front door, his son hanging dead in his arms. The father asked, 'Pastor, where's the resurrection now?' "

"But those parents—hard as it was—*still believed*. They were supported by a caring Christian community and their faith was strong. *They still believed in the resurrection*."

"I still can't understand how a little Jew on a cross 2,000 years ago has anything to do with me and my life today."

"Then why do we sit here today talking about him?"

Professor Karl Altenbrenner dug into his pizza—"the works," with anchovies on the side. Fresh salad, too. The clamor of the restaurant made him think of home. Vibrant young students. Academe. *His* world. He listened.

"You're giving us glib theological answers. If you had lived through the Holocaust, you'd speak differently!"

"The Holocaust. When we talk about six million Jews being killed, Bill, let's not forget twelve million other people! They're overlooked when we talk about mass murder. Genocide. Even twenty million Russian soldiers dying in the war! It's all hard to comprehend."

"But in the face of all that, how could Victor Frankl, a Jew, still come around to *hope* in his ultimate conclusions about everything?"

"And Eli Wiesel. You've read his *Night*, haven't you? A friend of mine, a black student at Pacific School of Religion in Berkeley, gave me a copy of her term paper this morning. It suggests his life is 'a model for refaithing.' He speaks of the progression of responses to the mass killing of his people: disbelief, anger, rebellion against God. Then, a void which signals aloneness and deep depression.

Suicide is considered. But then she says . . . and listen to this . . . and this is a *black* theologian writing about a *Jew's* faith *after* the Holocaust":

> Bargaining, concessions, and deals begin. Anything is better than having to live in a world that will not allow God, yet will not stand without God. The search for a means to reconcile the difference is the beginning of the reframing of faith necessary to begin spiritual life again. In the absence of God, others with God-like characteristics are found and confirm that God-ness exists. If faith in the traditional God is impossible then faith in the God-ness of some of humanity, at least, was a start. The one who has been in the dark night of the soul moves from the position of never-again to that of maybe-just-once. The emptiness of the night pushes, encourages and even demands another try.

"That's a black woman writing that?"

"Yeah."

"And you think she believes it—in the light of what has happened to her people?"

"Yeah. I know she does. She told me. She explained her views two weeks ago in a paper for Professor Harrison."

"Oh, look! Here's our pizza. One more paragraph, then let's eat."

"Refaithing flourishes in community . . . *Hope's Spring* is *eternal*. . . . Listen to this . . . 'There is more need for me to love God than to have God love me.' What makes the most sense to me is that there are many other brothers and sisters around the world who have shared with me, even at a distance, the dark night of the soul.' "

Karl shifted in his chair, as the theological student made his summation on Wiesel.

"And I think the most moving scene in *Night* is when two concentration camp inmates are watching that boy take one-half hour to die while hanging. 'Where is God now?' said the voice. And a voice within answered, 'Where is he? Here he is—he is hanging here on this gallows.' "

"Look, Hal," the student concluded, "I lost a brother in Vietnam. Where was God when they shot him down? I believe he was at the same place as he was when his Son died on the cross."

"That's a clever answer, my friend. But why doesn't God *speak*?

Why doesn't he *do* something about the hunger and hate and oppression in the world? Why is he forever *silent*?"

"Well, I'm trying to do something—in God's name. That's why I'm going into the ministry, although I believe *every profession* can be a 'ministry' for God."

"And the silence of God—as you and I see it—is still the silence *of* God. He's still there. The absence of evidence is not the evidence of absence."

Philosophy professor Karl Altenbrenner listened. He squinted his eyes and finished his last bite of pizza. He wiped his lips with the cheap paper napkin, and leaned back in his chair.

How he would love to get in on the conversation. But these were not his students. They could go on for hours, as his students had years before, with him "presiding". He had relished it. But now, he merely listened.

"But God must be 'willing' all this to happen. He lets it take place. I've heard many a Christian speak about an untimely, tragic death: 'It was *God's Will,*' they say."

"No!" responded another student quickly. "I don't buy that garbage. That's lousy theology. God doesn't will anyone's death. I think William Sloan Coffin put it very well the other day. His 24-year-old son drowned in his car in Boston Harbor. No drugs or booze. Just bad weather, no guard rail, or something like that. In his sermon ten days later at Riverside Church, Coffin said that God doesn't go around with his finger on triggers, his fist around knives, or his hands on steering wheels. In fact, Christ spent much of his time healing people. God didn't *will* his son's death. 'In fact,' Coffin said, 'when the waves closed over the sinking car, *God's was the first of all our hearts to break.*' "

"And he closed by saying that when the lamp of his son's life went out, it was because the Dawn had come for him."

Karl swallowed hard. A year ago the *Dawn* had come for his wife, Clara, also. The auto accident. Late one night a man who had fallen asleep at the wheel hit them head-on. She died instantly. He was hospitalized for months, immobile. First time like that in his life. Terminally ill, the man in the bed next to him was always so cheerful. Never argumentative, he had quietly shared his Christian faith with Karl. In further conversation he explained how confident he was about God's forgiveness and how thankful he was to God for everything in life.

What a courageous man! Always concerned about his grieving wife and kids. Blasted cheerful! Karl mused.

Then one day he was gone. When Karl awakened the man's bed was empty. He suddenly remembered an old story he had read about two other hospitalized men. The man near the window deftly described the view outside, a view the other man could not see—blooming flowers, children playing, seasonal changes—he did it so entrancingly. When he died, the man farther from the window asked to be taken over to it so he could see the view for himself. He gasped! No flowers, no children! Only a blank brick wall. The man had made it all up.

But not his *faith*. That was real. And he had described a possible scene outside the room of Karl's present life which was *not* a blank wall—but a whole new world of meaning he had never known before.

Karl had become a Christian then. He hadn't joined a church yet, or had any big conversion experience. He had known *about* the truths of Christianity for many years—and ridiculed them. But—slowly—he had seen Christ alive in a man next to him in that room for many months. He now knew the completeness and calm certainty of his faith. Karl had recognized the hollowness of his life. He had asked God's forgiveness. And God gave it to him. After that experience, things never looked the same to him again.

Karl smelled the pizza. The students were still shouting at each other. The warm sun felt good coming through his "window on the world." He smiled.

Sometimes God has to knock people down to their knees before they see fit to use them, Karl thought. *"Thank you, God, for another day."*

The intense conversation of the students continued.

"I still can't see it!" one of the Cal students said to a seminary student.

I didn't either, for a long time, Karl thought. How self-confident he had been! How many students had he disillusioned right in this very room!

From the conversation Karl sensed that outside again were the young students from Berkeley High mimicking British punks, always smoking, young boys spitting ostentatiously. Two coeds went by, one pushing the other (leg in a cast) in a wheelchair. The cast had at least 200 signatures on it in varied colors of ink. Another pair of older girls kissed as they parted to go to class. Their embrace was longer than usual.

Karl listened to the young students again.

"I still can't *see* it. It still just doesn't make sense to me."

"I know. I'm not trying to *prove* Christianity. I'm only explaining my own experience. Look, Hal. Some of the Fundamentalists on the Cal campus always try to *prove* Christianity. That's not where it's at. They say that Jesus either was what he claimed himself to be, the Son of God and the Savior of the world, *or* he was the greatest fraud, maniac, and liar the world has ever seen. And that it has to be one way or the other.

The sem student continued, "If I were an agnostic, that wouldn't convince me. I'd take a third alternative—simply that Jesus' disciples made it all up and later scribes added the stories about Jesus. No one *proves* the Christian faith. It has to be the work of God's Spirit in a person's heart. I believe in Christ because he has worked in my life. He forgives me even though I blow it every day. And that's not fatalism!" he added quickly, laughing. "God forgives me; he heals me; he gives me power to face each day."

His testimony continued, "I've met God personally in reading the Bible, in the fellowship of other Christians. They're just sinners as I am. I have seen the ambiguities, absurdities, and injustices in life. You know I spent a year in Mexico. But, despite what I say, I *still believe in God*. He created me. He gave me *life*—the very breath I'm using as I speak right now. But more important is God's great *forgiveness*—through *Christ's death on the cross and his resurrection*."

The room had quieted down now. Many students had left for afternoon classes. The group at the table behind Karl had also heard the theological student's final words.

"Nice sermon, Reverend," one young student stated. "But you're not living in today's world. This is the twentieth century. We have to be realistic! I've gotta go. I'm due back at the lab. I guess you want all of us Cal pagans to take that great 'leap of faith' you Christians are always taking about?"

"Bill, it's not a *blind* leap, or a gullible faith. For us, it's not a leap into the dark, but a leap into the hands of a loving, forgiving God. Because he's said he'll be there. I know. I took the jump three years ago. *God is there.*"

The student quickly added, "In fact, the God you are rejecting is not my God at all. Remember how in Heller's *Catch 22* Captain Yossarian tried to bed down with Lt. Scheisskopf's wife. He called God a clumsy, bungling, brainless, conceited, uncouth hayseed for not doing a better job with the universe. The woman burst into tears and screamed at him to stop. And he asked why she was so upset, because he believed she didn't believe in God herself. She said she didn't, but that the God she didn't believe in is a 'good God, a just God, a merciful God, not the mean and stupid God he made God out to be.' "

The sem student summarized, "It's a great scene. You say Christians simply make a wish-projection of the kind of a God they want. I say you are rejecting a God of *your* own fabrication and have never really met the God I know, the God you *can* get to know."

"Sorry, gotta split," said another student. "Too bad Yossarian didn't make out with Mrs. Scheisskopf!" The student bowed dramatically and disappeared out the pizzeria door. The Campanile bells sounded 2 p.m.

As the noisy students began to leave, so did Professor Karl Altenbrenner. How like himself—and other students he had known in years past! They were energetic, self-convinced, blind to truths other than those they had experienced in life. So *closed.*

How blind he had been, and how sightlessly dogmatic in his "brilliant" philosophy classes. He had presented only one point of view after all—skepticism.

And then, after the accident, how differently he saw things.

He arose from his chair and stepped out into the aisle, inadvertently knocking over a chair.

"Hey, why don't you look where you're going!" a student yelled at him.

"I'm sorry," the Professor said. "I don't see things the way I used to."

"Oh," said the student. And for the first time he saw the old man's white cane.

The Long, Dark Tunnel

A Physicist Meets a Skeptical Young Woman on an Alpine Train

At 6:40 a.m. Hulda Hohenstein boarded the train in Interlaken, Switzerland. Her destination was the Jungfrau, high atop the Swiss Alps.

She looked at the other passengers. Most of them worked at hotels in little villages along the way, or at the Jungfrau restaurant. Outside, a young woman ran toward the train. She climbed aboard just as the train pulled out, on time, at 6:42 a.m. Breathlessly she sat down in a seat facing Hulda. Panting, she exclaimed, "Just made it! My name is Maria."

"I'm Hulda."

The young woman was pretty, simply dressed, probably in her mid-twenties. But pain was written across her face.

Hulda noted that most of the other occupants of the car were locals. The tourists, having slept late, would take the more crowded, late-morning departure.

The electric train glided smoothly through the fields with their newly-mown hay. Hulda enjoyed its exotic freshness.

As the train crossed the narrow streets leaving Interlaken, Hulda heard the "ding-ding-ding" of the crossing barriers. A small *Ferienwohnung*, a vacation hotel, called "Orion," slipped by outside the window. Cattle, carrying huge clanging bells under their massive necks, sidled away from the passing train which had picked up its speed. Hulda noted a family of young children, parents, and grandparents pitch hay into old wooden wagons.

The trip would take approximately two hours to the top. The mood was set by the silence as the riders eyed each other carefully. Across from Hulda, the young woman had now relaxed. Hulda smiled at her. As the train sped along, Hulda became so engrossed in the beautiful, familiar scenery, she was surprised when they neared Lauterbrunnen.

"Oh, there it is!" she exclaimed to the young woman, who turned to join her as they viewed a magnificent waterfall drifting gently down hundreds of feet from high on the mountain.

"Have you ever traveled above Lauterbrunnen, to Mürren?" Hulda inquired politely.

"No. I'm not too fond of taking those trams through the sky!"

"I understand. But once you're there it's just like being close to heaven itself. You're completely cut off from the world. No cars. Quiet. *Wunderbar*!"

Additional passengers boarded. The train began the climb to Wengwald and Wengen.

Viewing the bright mountain flowers on both sides of the tracks, Hulda exclaimed, "God made such gorgeous flowers in the high country!"

Maria Kurtz looked coolly at Hulda. "I don't believe in God," she announced firmly. Both fell into silence for a while.

But there was something about this kindly old woman seated across from her that made Maria relent a little. She could at least be polite to her.

Maria looked Hulda over again. She appeared to be in her mid-sixties, making her forty years older than Maria. Maria wondered what she would look like at that age. Would she pull back her graying hair into a tiny bun? Hulda wore a neat gray suit. But what captivated Maria's attention were the woman's eyes—blue and clear and smiling.

They exchanged a few pleasantries and Maria felt more and more at ease with the woman. There was a certain radiant, relaxed cheerfulness which drew her to the woman.

"I didn't mean to be rude a few minutes ago when I said I didn't believe in God. Frankly," she sighed, "I don't believe in men, either!" She frowned and laughed at the same time.

And then, somehow, Maria's whole story came out. It was good to talk about it to someone—finally. Her folks were dead, she often felt lonely. "You are so kind," she told Hulda. "I feel I can talk to you, even though you are a stranger."

She and her husband, Gunther, had grown up in Addleswill, on the outskirts of Zurich. They had fallen in love and enrolled at the University of Zurich together. He majored in philosophy, and she in music.

Gunther and Maria had gone to church in their youth. But at

Zurich they had become part of a fascinating intellectual crowd. Maria described its scintillation to Hulda.

"The friends we made were 'hedonists of the mind'," she added and went on to describe how they demanded a lot of each other in their various disciplines. They always had to be on their toes.

There was a powerful athleticism—of the body as well as the mind. They would get fantastic natural 'highs' from strenuous exercise after spending hours over books or in the lab.

But what really turned them on was *achievement*—not for money, but for its own sake. They sought to stretch the limits of human potentiality. They had no illusions about the meaninglessness of life. They quoted Camus or Sartre endlessly. God was irrelevant to them.

They were truly intellectually interested in *ideas*. There was a certain secular joy in *humanness*. They were pleased with a friend's achievement—or at being beaten at one's own game—and enjoying it.

Maria talked rapidly, animatedly, recalling her days at the university. Then she grew silent. She looked out the windows of the train and noticed they had stopped briefly in Wengen. Huge, ornate old hotels loomed up above twisted streets. She saw horse-drawn buggies and bicycles scattered near the station.

As the train started, Hulda watched Maria quietly. She saw a shadow cross her face.

"But I'm all out of that now," she told Hulda. "My husband Gunther left me—for another woman—my best friend! I didn't think that could ever happen to me. But it did. Gunther is a confirmed agnostic now.

"And I guess I'm one, too," she added. "How could a loving God let that happen to me?"

Maria looked out at the still-visible waterfall of Lauterbrunnen, even more spectacular at a distance.

"I worked nights in a fondue restaurant in downtown Zurich. I tried to keep our bills paid. Then I learned he was not home studying but was out with *her*!"

Hulda listened quietly.

"So I lost my husband. I have no money. I heard about a job opening as waitress at the Jungfraujoch restaurant, at the top of the mountain. I grabbed for it. Anything to get away. There's no music left in my heart. Here I am—no husband, no future, and no God who cares. No, I can't believe in a good and loving God any more."

Hulda had said nothing for a long time, except for a faint echoing sigh as Maria told her story. "I cannot know the pain you have been through, Maria," she said softly. "but I am sorry. Ah, look! We're nearing *Kleine Scheidegg*!"

Soon the train stopped, and since they had a few minutes before catching a different train, Maria and Hulda wandered through the shops near the little station. They were on a great plateau bathed in bright sunlight. It was a glorious day, unlike some which started out clear in Interlaken but often ended in disappointment when the train reached the top and a dismayed band of a hundred or so tourists found themselves unable to see anything outside the restaurant—because of a blinding blizzard.

But today was enchanting. Far below, passengers saw Interlaken nestled in the valley like a toy village. Above them towered the Jungfrau, its cap gleaming white in the radiant sun.

Several workers in the *Kleine Scheidegg* restaurant and shops had left the train, so Maria and Hulda found themselves together in the back of an almost empty car.

The train began the long uphill course that headed for the tunnel and the Jungfrau—a forty-five minute run through solid rock.

"You know," Maria studied Hulda intently, "I feel I've seen you somewhere before."

"I'm at the university, too," Hulda replied.

"What do you do there?" Maria asked, envisioning her as one of other elderly women who scrubbed day after day, keeping the tiled halls immaculate.

"I teach in the Physics Department."

"Hohenstein—*Doctor* Hohenstein!"

"Yes."

"The famous physicist!"

Hulda said nothing. Maria's jaw dropped.

"And you believe in God?"

"Of course," Hulda replied softly.

Silence followed for a moment as Maria reappraised the woman sitting across from her.

She noted the brown age spots on the woman's delicate hands, the frailness of her body, the wrinkles in her kind face. Somehow they added to the latent dignity of the woman.

Dr. Hulda Hohenstein—the renowned physicist! Sitting just across from her!

Hulda was also lost in her own thoughts as her mind went back to another place and another time when she, too, had struggled with the faith. It happened at the university when she and Karl were young. She had doubts, plenty of them. She recalled what C. S. Lewis had so aptly said: "The great Angler played His fish and I never dreamed that the hook was in my tongue."

She and Karl had married. But then it happened.

Hulda swallowed hard and looked out at *Kleine Scheidegg* now far below. They would soon be in *the long, dark tunnel.*

Hulda decided to tell Maria her story.

She had met Karl at a pizza parlor near the university. They had fallen in love. They had married in the *Reformierte Kirche* on the square in Interlaken and stayed at the nearby Europa Hotel. They had walked arm-in-arm along the lakeshore of the nearby *Brienzersee* in the cool of the evening. Their honeymoon had been an idyllic week of discovering how deep and lasting their love was.

And then, just before they were to return to Zurich, they took a trip up to the *Jungfraujoch*. They sat in the old hotel (which later burned down), drank dark German beer, and looked out at the 20-mile long glacier that spread out before them.

They heard the mountain climbers come back at noon, their spiked boots ringing down the long hallways, their faces flushed red by snowburn and the pride in having conquered the Fenster or the Eiger, or the Jungfrau, which towered above the Joch. And they had walked out on the *Ewigeschneefeld*—the eternal snow field, 1300 feet deep, which saddled the majestic peaks. They had watched the guide with his Eskimo Huskies guiding tourists along the safe, well-marked path.

But it was there it happened. The fog had blanketed them quickly. Hulda had walked a few feet ahead of Karl to the entrance to the Joch. In seconds the fog separated them. Karl had called to her, but the wind raised its voice also.

Within an hour they knew. He had wandered off the path and fallen into a crevice.

He was gone. Somewhere deep in the ice and snow. His body

would not come out for years—decades — at the end of the glacier.

Forty years ago! Hulda pulled herself back to reality, and looked at Maria's pale, drawn face.

"And so I am coming up here again," she added. "Last night I went down to the church by the square to pray. Today is our wedding anniversary. I come up once a year—in Karl's remembrance."

Maria blanched. "But—*you still believe in God*? After *that*!"

"Of course. In fact, my faith is stronger than it was before."

"But . . . " stammered Maria. "How?"

"Suffering. It draws a person closer to God. It's hard to explain *how*. No one wants pain or loss. But through it God brings us closer to himself in Jesus Christ. He makes us more dependent upon him and *his* strength."

The train ground slowly through the black tunnel on a steep angle. Hulda leaned back against the hard wooden seat and continued.

"Look at Job, in the Old Testament. He lost everything he had. *Everything*. Sure, he questioned God for a while, and his friends tried to undermine his faith. But in the end 'Job placed his hand upon his lips'."

Hulda had moved her hand up to her aging, thin lips, as she spoke.

"Job realized that *God is God*. He doesn't have to fit into our puny conceptions of him. We need not question him. He is the *creator*. We are the *creatures*."

"But it just doesn't make sense," Maria countered firmly.

"Faith isn't 'sense'," said Hulda. "It's believing. You can't argue with faith. It's a gift of God."

Warming to the subject, Hulda continued, "You could put it the way a colleague of mine does at the University. He's a renowned political philosopher, *and* a practicing Christian. He claims he returned to Christianity because the Christian faith was the only thing that made sense! He said if life is not a drama of salvation it is nothing. He says he sees the evil in himself and in humanity from which we must be redeemed. For him, for me, for many in the intellectual community, Christ Jesus personifies and embodies that salvation."

"You don't blame God for your husband's death, then?" Maria asked, puzzled.

"No," Hulda answered, as she looked at the large gold ring on her finger. "God didn't 'call Karl home'. Death claims us all. We are all sinners. God didn't 'call Karl home'. But he was waiting for Karl when he got there."

"It's mind-boggling for me that you can believe the way you do. And you—a scientist!"

"I see no contradiction at all. The 'truths' I teach are God's truths. They originated from *his* creative hand. He has let us discover some of them. I believe we'll discover others. The more we learn in physics the more we realize how little we know—and how vast God is."

Maria exclaimed, "But I just can't see where you get the strength to carry on."

"It's not *my* strength, Maria, but God in Christ, in me."

Hulda paused a moment. "Maria, do you read your Bible? Do you have any Christian friends?"

"No—on both counts, I must say."

"You can't be a Christian in a vacuum, Maria," Hulda said softly. "When you seek God, he will let you find him. He's there, in his Word, and the Sacraments if you search for him there. Like the electricity for this train, it has to be hooked up to the power supply far from us."

Both women remained silent for a long time. The train climbed more steeply into the darkness ahead.

Maria could hardly believe that sitting quietly in front of her was an old woman, but a famous physicist whose husband was frozen solid up there somewhere in a crevice in a 1300-foot deep ice and snow pack. She recalled the Swiss German word for "calving," how after decades a body would pop out twenty miles away at the end of the glacier.

There it would be—frozen ageless from a point in its youth long ago.

She could picture Karl—handsome, blond—and Hulda today—aged Hulda.

How weird! But God let it happen!

What a faith this woman has! Maria marvelled.

Suddenly Maria wasn't so sure about what she didn't believe. Without thinking, she blurted out, "Dr. Hohenstein . . ."

"Hulda. . . ."

"All right, Hulda. Will you pray for me?"

"Of course," Hulda responded. "But I thought you weren't sure about Christianity any more."

"Well, after talking to you I'm not so sure . . . that I'm not sure!" Maria laughed. "That came out rather badly, didn't it?"

They both laughed.

"You know, Maria, even our famous Swiss Christian physician, Paul Tournier, tells a story that fits with what you just said," Hulda commented as she proceeded to fill in the details. Reared an orphan, Tournier experienced trouble accepting himself and being accepted by other people. But a Greek professor took an interest in him, and that helped.

The professor was not a Christian, but he invited Tournier into his home and into his intellectual world.

Some years later, after Tournier had become a Christian, he visited his old friend again. He was looking for someone to critique a manuscript before sending it to a publisher. So he had come to the retired professor-friend.

He asked Tournier to read the manuscript aloud for him. At the end of each chapter, Tournier looked to his old friend for comments, but the old professor simply said, "Paul, keep reading."

After this had happened several times, the teacher said, "Paul, we must pray together." And so they prayed.

Later Tournier exclaimed, "I didn't know you were a Christian!"

"Yes, I am," his friend replied.

"Well, when did you become a Christian?"

"Just now," his friend answered.

Again there was the silence between Hulda and Maria, but it was now an easy, relaxed silence, settling around them like a friend.

"I don't think it will be that way for me," said Maria finally, "*if* I ever come back to God."

"Of course not," affirmed Hulda. "The path back to God is different for each one of us. But Christ leads the way. Through him we are assured that there is *light at the end of the tunnel.*"

Maria studied the tiny lines around Hulda's mouth. Suddenly they disappeared as a broad grin lit up Hulda's face.

"You want to hear another story—well, really a conversation?"

Hulda asked, her blue eyes twinkling, and in a few phrases told the story.

A young student at the university went to see a Lutheran pastor who was working on his degree in modern German literature. In his office she said, "I'm an atheist."

He replied, "Well, tell me what kind of a God you don't believe in."

And for an hour she told him. When the hour was up, the young pastor said, "That's very interesting; but you know, I must be an atheist, too, because I don't believe in that God, either!"

And then he told her about a *different* kind of God than the one she had envisioned.

"The point is," Hulda summarized, "so many people have never known the God they *say* they are rejecting. But the *real* God—God's kind of God—is big enough to cope with the most brilliant person's rejection of him. Though God gives us life itself—and we misuse it when we 'play God'—he also gives us forgiveness through Christ's death on the cross—and resurrection. Wonder of wonders!"

"I wish I could have a faith like that," said Maria softly.

"You can," Hulda said. "Just ask him. I believe he's been waiting to hear from you."

"Oh, my goodness! We're here!" Hulda suddenly gasped.

The train came to a jerky halt. They got down out of the car. A huge sign greeted them: *Jungfrau—11,111 feet above sea level.*

Maria grasped Hulda's hands. She felt a firm response.

"I . . . I just don't know quite what to say . . . Thank you so much. I so enjoyed meeting you."

"Remember, Maria, you're always welcome at my home in Zurich."

"You can be sure, I'll remember. I'll see you again, Hulda!"

"Auf wiedersehen!"

"Auf wiedersehen!"

Maria headed quickly for the restaurant in the *Jungfraujoch*, and Hulda began the long walk down the tunnel that led to the outside.

She opened the door and stepped out on the *Ewigeschneefeld*—the eternal snowfield. There stood the guide with his Eskimo Huskies. No tourists yet. Deep down, beneath her feet, in the sleep of death, hard in the ice and snow, lay her Karl.

Requiescat in pace, Karl. Rest in peace.

Hulda looked up. Massive yellow clouds hung over the end of the glacier as if suddenly placed there as a replica of a master's painting in the Louvre.

She looked heavenward at the Jungfrau and the bright blue sky behind.

Maria's words came back—"I'll see you again."

"And I will see you again, Karl," spoke Hulda softly. "But not here."

II

DIALOG

Our odyssey now leads to examining contemporary approaches to educated adults in and outside the church. Chapter 4 includes the characteristics of the educated and implications for ministering to them. Succeeding chapters deal with preaching to the educated, Bible study, the use of the case method, and finally how a trust-relationship with the educated might be established.

4

Characteristics of the Educated Adult: Implications for the Church's Ministry

P. T. Forsyth has said:

> What is indicated therefore is not that the manner of the Gospel which is most engaging and welcome to the world should necessarily give the type for the church, but that what God has given us as the type for the church should go to the world in the most engaging and welcome way.[1]

In a study paper for my course, James T. Oldham analyzed the characteristics of the educated adult as he observed them. The rest of this chapter, except for bracketed editorial comments, is a reproduction of Oldham's analysis, together with his suggestions for ministering to the educated.[2]

Characteristic 1: Superior Intelligence

This is probably the most obvious, though not necessarily the most significant, characteristic of the educated adult. Although there are variations from person to person, educated adults tend to score higher on tests of intelligence. They have extensive vocabularies and read at a level significantly above that of the average person. They possess higher than average verbal and quantitative abilities and they tend to prefer abstract to concrete thinking. They tend to be more influenced by logic than by emotion and tend to be quite functional in spotting inconsistencies and weaknesses in argumentation and organization. For all these reasons, they tend to do very well in academic work and settings. They will normally have completed formal education to the maximum level commensurate with their ability and finances and will generally be committed to a lifelong adventure of continuing education.

The most significant implication of this characteristic is that we must be prepared to present the option of the Christian faith at a level commensurate with their intellectual ability and academic achievement. It is important to demonstrate, both in word and by example, that Christianity is not just a crutch for the uneducated or a life option reserved for the simplistic. Wherever possible, those who work with the educated in education and evangelism should have equivalent levels of ability, understanding, and achievement, or at least not be threatened, intimidated, or hostile to academic achievement.

[Parenthetically, it ought to be noted here that superior or inferior intelligence actually plays little or no role in coming to the faith. Intelligence alters the setting; yet it does not alter the fact that false gods must be sacrificed and done to death before either the super intelligent or the not-so-intelligent can be drawn into the faith; and the latter may hang onto their false gods with stronger arguments than the former in individual instances.]

The work of Christian apologetics will be very important here since the educated will tend to raise intellectual objections to Christianity that will not concern or bother other people. The worker with the educated adult should be very well acquainted with this field and be prepared to share and recommend helpful resources. On the other hand, it is impossible to prove the truth of Christianity by argumentation and logic; for repentance, belief, and commitment are, in the end, acts of faith. Therefore, a key concept to stress in working with the educated adult is that faith, while not irrational, is something suprarational; ultimately we look for some, but not all, of its claims to be verified existentially, rather than seeking victory now in logical debate.

Characteristic 2: Cultural Immersion

Educated adults tend to depend heavily on classical and contemporary art, music, drama, literature, and other print media for their information, aesthetic stimulation, and worldview. They are much more widely read and schooled in the cultural milieu than the average person. They tend to buy hardback books, go to plays and concerts, have tastefully decorated homes, and subscribe to and support public (cultural) television. They tend to have a lot less respect and interest in the popular media, such as TV, radio, and movies, than their less educated contemporaries. Because of this characteristic, they tend to be much better acquainted with the real lifestyles, agonies, and struggles of modern man than most church people who invest most of their time, energy, and cultural investment in the evangelical ghettos of Christian broadcasting, Christian bookstores, and exclusively Christian groups and experiences.

As we seek to reach the educated adult, we too must be intimately acquainted with the cultural sources that define their frame of reference. We must be reading more than the Bible, so we can be prepared to cite and to say how its truth may intersect with the life and needs of modern man and woman. We must also find ways to make a witness felt in these areas and media of culture where the anti-intellectualism of Jimmy Swaggart, the syrup of Evie, and the neat packages of Billy Graham films will not always gain an audience, let alone sell.

Characteristic 3: Integrative Thinking

By virtue of their training and background, educated adults tend to be well-acquainted with a broad spectrum of the liberal arts including philosophy, history, psychology, sociology, literature, and current events. Their understandings and interpretations of religion and Christianity will not exist in a vacuum from their learnings in these fields of knowledge. Even more important, they have been taught and accepted a methodology that emphasizes the cruciality of being able to integrate learning from various fields to come up with holistic and true perceptions of the world in which they live. Thus, whatever messages come to them through the church and its writers, preachers, and teachers will be subjected to this mental integrative grid that is very active and prominent in their minds.

In working with the educated, therefore, it is most urgent that we not appear to be in opposition to either the technical or social sciences but rather in concert with them in attempt to discover truth wherever it may be found, for ultimately "all truth is God's truth." We should stress the positive relationship between Christianity and these scientific disciplines. We can draw heavily on them for insights that undergird the Christian message and also point to ways that faith may impinge upon, enrich, and even improve their teachings and practices. The works of thoughtful Christians now seeking to forge a synthesis between faith and another discipline can be very helpful at this point. A good example among current thinkers is M. Scott Peck, whose writings are lifting up the congruence between religious understandings and psychology and psychiatry.

[Given M. Scott Peck's reputation in the psychiatric community, some would consider him a problematic example, though he does strive for an integration of the Biblical with a discipline. I believe that it is important for the Christian to use the academic disciplines for all they are worth. Note, however, that the conceptual framework of certain disciplines at specific points in history do act as agents of the culture's basic lies and idols. Therefore, critical, Biblically-based evaluation is the order of the day.]

Characteristic 4: A Thirst for Relevance

Along with many other adults, but with particular force and urgency, the educated are concerned to see that religious faith is really relevant to their lives and their society. This characteristic does present a real challenge to much of the ministry of the church that seems steeped in tradition, esoteric doctrinal differences, and an Ancient-Near-East culture and worldview.

As Jerold W. Apps puts it,

> These people want a church that is interested in this life, this world. They won't accept a church that only instructs them for salvation. They want a church that helps them to meet the everyday problems of living, how to cope with family tensions, how to communicate with teenagers. They want a church that's concerned with the problems of society, drug abuse, civil rights, war, population control. These are problems the church can help solve.[3]

So it does not have to be this way. The Christian faith can be presented as something relevant to every aspect of one's life and work and the concerns of today's society rather than a "Sunday-only" or "heavenly-only" type of reality. As many have argued, we have a Biblical and historical foundation for such a holistic presentation, if we can only recover that foundation from the privatization and spiritualization to which Christianity has been so heavily subject in this twentieth century. Robert Clemmons lifts up this vision of relevant Christian proclamation:

> If the Christian religion is to be presented in understandable form, it is imperative that a curriculum have a design for its meanings that is comprehensive. It must include man's relation to God as creator who is active in human history. It must include man's relation to man so that persons may discover the meaning of being human, the ethical purposes guiding man's relation to his fellowmen. It must include man's relation to the world which manifests God's providence and in which man is steward.[4]

It is certain that if we wish to reach the educated, the content of our witness must be this inclusive. Our methodology should also emphasize relevance. King James English and traditional religious jargon are counterproductive. The use of modern translations of scripture, contemporary Christian writers, and non-traditional religious language is much more likely to create a response in the educated adult. It is easier and more comprehensible, for example, to urge people to allow God to help them to become all that he intends for them to be than it is to demand that they be "sanctified in the Spirit."

Characteristic 5: Philosophically Open

Educated adults have a philosophical commitment to research, testing, experimentation, open discussion, analysis, and critique, and empirical evidence as the final validators of truth. They have been brought up on the scientific method which insists nothing is true or certain just because someone claims that it is, but because it can be empirically demonstrated as true. They are also conditioned to regard all truth, even when empirically established, as tentative, subject to further research and refinement or redefinition.

With this in mind, it is vital to avoid claiming divine revelation and indisputability for tangential aspects of faith or something which is only speculation. This does not mean that the essence of the Gospel cannot be proclaimed with heart and fervor, but the essence does not consist in the nature of the millennium, the correct mode of baptism, or the acceptability of alcohol consumption, our intransigence on which often turns off philosophically open adults before they ever get to the basic claims of Christ on their lives.

This characteristic also suggests that in the presentation of the Gospel message, it is desirable to present the beliefs, claims, and promises of Christianity as tenets to be explored and investigated rather than closed issues and to challenge the openness of the educated adult to the invitation of Jesus Christ. In this way, we can see and use the philosophical openness of the education as a predisposition to faith rather than an inherent barrier to it. Father John Powell uses this style of presentation as a most effective introduction to his book *A Reason to Live! A Reason to Die! A New Look at Faith in God*.

[A caution should be injected here. Intellectuals, Christian and non-Christian, claim to be philosophically open and may truly believe that they are. In dealing with the educated we should therefore appeal to their *alleged* openness. Many educated adults are not truly philosophically open. Many do not even recognize the difference in epistemological systems—a key to true openness. Therefore we do well to point out that even in daily life the empirical method is not the only way of knowing we employ. This has far-ranging implications for our Christian witness.]

Characteristic 6: Tolerant of Diversity

This characteristic is an axiom of the preceding one. Since the educated tend to remain open about truth until it is conclusively demonstrated, they tend to be much more comfortable with and tolerant of a diversity of opinions, possibilities, and alternatives than the average person in society. Those who are less secure in themselves may be looking for an authoritarian voice to give them "the answer" but this does not include the educated. The educated tend to view premature foreclosure of option and possibilities as defensiveness and destructive in effect since it may prematurely eliminate a possible correct answer, interpretation, or course of action.

Once again this suggests that our style with the educated should be self-assured, non-defensive, and non-threatened. We certainly have nothing to hide and nothing to fear from the most careful scrutiny of our understandings and those of other faiths and perspectives. In working with the educated it is wise to present options for interpretation and alternatives for action rather than fixed answers wherever possible. We should also encourage discussion, dialog, and debate as helpful and effective methods for conversion and growth.

[Keep in mind the caution noted under Characteristic 5. The educated person wishes to be tolerant of diversity and may truly attempt to be flexible. That is important, even though the educated may not be able to be consistent in that respect.]

Characteristic 7: Universalistic

Because of their openness, tolerance of diversity, and ability to stand outside of themselves to see another's perspective, there is a strong tendency for the educated to be universalistic in their views about religion and salvation. They will be quick to see the similarities among various religious faiths and question if there is not some kernel of truth that unites and stands behind each of them in spite of cultural, linguistic, and traditional differences. They will also project their tolerance of religious differences onto God and conclude that he finds them equally acceptable and their adherents equally worthy of blessing and paradise.

The question of universalism is, of course, a profoundly deep and difficult theological question. The consensus of Christian thinking, however, is that it is essential to lift up certain particular claims of Christianity as definitive and to reject a complete and total universalism. This could be one of the more serious points of tension or disagreement between the church and the educated. The most positive approach seems to be in these steps:

a. Acknowledge genuine points of congruence between Christianity and other faiths. It only diverts attention and interest to create differences where they really do not exist. Moreover, certain universal similarities with respect to religious faith may make a rather persuasive apologetic argument to the educated.

b. Affirm the concern that wishes that "all might be saved and come to the knowledge of the truth" as a divine one.

c. Tactfully point out the meaningful differences which do exist between Christianity and its rival religions.

d. Stress the potential negative impact of a total universalist position, particularly on such issues as sin and evil, moral discrimination, fellowship with God, and existential commitment.

Characteristic 8: Nonauthoritarian

As suggested by several of the previous characteristics, the educated are not only non-authoritarian in style and disposition themselves, but they also tend to resist violently authoritarianism in others. They look to both individuals and organizations, such as preachers and the church, to establish their authority through demonstrated competence and moral suasion rather than the authoritarian wielding of power or clever manipulation of ideas and people. If we come across to these people as "Take or leave it," "turn or burn," or "It's so because the church says so," we will probably both lose their interest and arouse their antagonism at the same time.

Therefore, it is important that we deemphasize authoritarian attitudes and styles in our education and evangelism with the educated. This will not be as easy as it sounds because the witness of the church has tended to be rather authoritarian through the centuries. However, in our work with the educated we need to establish and maintain credibility through calm self-assurance, integrity, genuine compassion, and reliance on the Holy Spirit. As we look to the Scriptures we may indeed find that it was these very elements that gave Jesus' teaching its "authority."

[While the intellectual strives towards non-authoritarianism, in the final analysis, perhaps no one is completely successful in that respect. Press the instructor far enough and you will probably find the issues that may not be treated "objectively" in the classroom, for instance. A typical example might be an instructor who would allow a debate over race, including racist points of view, but who would not allow a debate over AIDS, abortion, and other social issues. Christians are only authoritarian on different issues than the "objective" intellectual; it is really not a question of one's being nonauthoritarian and the other not. Of course, the theological explanation for the failings of the intellectual and/or the Christian lies in human nature and the continuing, innate sinful tendencies of every human being.]

Characteristic 9: Motivated by Service Needs

In the terms of psychologist Abraham Maslow, the educated in our society tend to have successfully fulfilled most of their lower levels of need (such as safety and security) and have moved on to needs at a higher point in Maslow's hierarchy (such as esteem, aesthetic, actualization, and service). The Christian Gospel, of course, speaks to each level of need with a different aspect of God's good news. But it makes little sense to address a Gospel presentation to the educated from a perspective where they do not, or no longer, sense a need. It is a waste of time and counterproductive to try to create a need where it does not exist; and the educated will usually recognize this technique for the manipulation that it is.

What we need to do is to scratch them where they itch—present the claims of the Gospel as they particularly meet the well-educated and financially and psychologically secure members of society. One thinks of Jesus' encounter with the rich young ruler. Jesus identified his sin not so much in terms of specific acts as in terms of a wasting of potential for service and further personal growth. This approach will hit many of the educated right where they are, and they may follow Jesus first into service and later into a true appreciation of salvation, contrary to our normal expectations and desires. It is true that they may not always respond, even as the rich young ruler did not, but at least they will have had the opportunity to experience a genuine Gospel challenge tailored to their needs in life.

Characteristic 10: Self-Directed in Learning

In the process of becoming educated, adults have been taught not only specific academic content, but also the process of learning itself, irrespective of the field or area of endeavor. They have not only been trained to locate needed information, expert opinion, and resources, both printed and personal, but they have even developed skills in determining what it is they need to learn and how effectively they are proceeding to any particular learning objective. These are pretty advanced abilities with which the church educator must interface in comparison with the skills and attitudes that many less educated adults bring to the church education setting. However, we ought not to look at this as a negative; for as Bergevin and McKinley point out, these are the very characteristics that can optimize learning:

> If we are to learn most effectively, we adults must ourselves discover and recognize a personal reason for learning about a given topic. It is not enough for someone to tell us why he thinks it is important for us to learn a certain thing. Learning programs should begin and deal with needs which learners recognize as needs. This condition can be met most satisfactorily when we learners become actively involved in some way in planning and evaluating the educational experience. . . . We can best become responsible for our learning if we participate in some way.[5]

The obvious conclusion is that in working with educated adults we should involve them as fully as possible in the planning, conducting, and evaluation of their learning experiences. We should take advantage of their skills in educational planning and resourcing and involve them wherever possible as teachers, librarians and resource developers, program planners, and advisors in other educational capacities. We should also recognize the usefulness and effectiveness of more individualized settings and techniques for learning on the part of the educated adult.

Characteristic 11: Oriented to Variety

Because of the great diversity of styles of learning to which well-educated adults have been exposed and because they themselves realize that different types of learning are better facilitated by different techniques, the educated prefer much more diversity and innovation in the style and content of programming, services, and learning experiences than will probably be true for most people in a given congregation or community. Because of their mental ability and openness to diversity, they can easily move from a lecture presentation to a film to a role-play to a debate or open discussion, and they will expect to make these kinds of moves as dictated by the situation and learning objectives, or they may easily become bored and restless. The same may not be true for adults generally who may prefer continuity in style and become disoriented or even angry if there are even small changes in the ways things are done.

The reality is that if we are going to meaningfully involve educated adults in religious programming, we must offer a variety of programs tailored to their time schedules, lifestyles, and learning preferences rather than expecting or requiring them to fit into the way "we've always done it." This may mean special classes, options within classes, some innovation in established groups, and/or personalized instruction and involvement. The needs of others must be considered as well, of course, but they too should be helped to see how everyone might benefit from changes, improvements and innovations from time to time.

Characteristic 12: Critical of and Impatient with Waste

The educated are apt to be quite critical and impatient with waste of any type—whether it be waste of money, time, or energy. They tend to be busy people with many commitments and relationships which extend beyond the circle of the church or Christian community. Because of their education and training, they tend to be professionals and respected leaders in the community. In their background and training, they have been exposed to quality educational and cultural experiences. They are unlikely to be very pleased or tolerant of church programs or activities that seem to be boring repetitions, senseless get-togethers, and nonsensical busy work. They are likely to be involved not out of tradition, habit, or institutional loyalty but only when they perceive it is really worth their time and effort to be involved. With respect to most church programming, they believe they could make better use of their time and, quite frankly, they could.

This suggests that in our outreach to the educated, quality must be emphasized in all aspects of programming and ministry, particularly the areas of leadership and resource development. Quality is a much more important factor than quantity, and this can be readily observed in the schedule of congregations and religious groups that appeal to well-educated members of our society. It is also essential that requests for time and talent involvement should relate to meaningful and not routine or counterproductive institutional maintenance tasks. Looked at another way, emphasis with the educated adult should be on the scattering function, rather than the gathering one, since they are already well-scattered and in positions to make a significant Christian impact if we don't brainwash them with the idea that their Christian commitment requires primarily a commitment to be at the church building whenever the doors are open.

Characteristic 13: Prejudiced against Faith

As a final descriptive characteristic, it should be noted that educated adults will be more prone to be prejudiced against faith as a valid and constructive option in their own life or in the life of society. This reservation (or even hostility) may be due to their own personal experience of faith which may be limited to very closed, judgmental, fundamentalistic, legalistic, and/or anti-intellectual expressions. It may also be related to a rather keen awareness of the defects of Christianity as it has taken concrete expression in various historical circumstances and settings.

It is important that we accept these feelings of prejudice as the educated may bring them to us, without defensiveness or panic. While admitting to some of the problems involved in the actual expression of the Christian faith, it is not necessary for us to make common league with the educated in a fruitless and non-constructive attack on the people or institutions involved. Rather it behooves us to help the educated to understand, as their perceptive ability should easily allow them to if sufficiently motivated, the *Sitz im Leben* of those involved in these less than adequate expressions of the Gospel of Christ. At the same time, we can model and lift up for them in our words, attitudes, and example, a Christianity that is more tolerant, intellectually honest, more liberating and humane than these which they may have previously been acquainted with or even attacked by.

Conclusion

Reaching the educated adult in our society will not be easy. However, the more we tailor our ministry efforts to the recognized characteristics of this special and vital target group, the more effective our efforts will be, and we may be assured, like the apostle Paul, that we will indeed save many.

Common Characteristics of the Educated Adult	**Implications for the Church's Ministry of Evangelism and Education**
SUPERIOR INTELLIGENCE	
1. Have extensive vocabularies; possess higher than average verbal and quantitative abilities; prefer abstract to concrete thinking.	1. Present Christian faith option at a level commensurate with their academic achievement; be prepared to deal with intellectual objections to faith, but also to interpret the nature of faith as a suprarational reality.
CULTURAL IMMERSION	
2. Tend to depend more on art, music, drama, literature, and other print media and less on popular mass media (radio, TV, movies) for their information and worldview.	2. Need to be well acquainted with these sources so that we can understand their frame of reference.
INTEGRATIVE THINKING	
3. Are well acquainted with a broad spectrum of the liberal arts including philosophy, history, psychology, sociology, literature, and current events; interdisciplinary in their thinking.	3. Stress the positive relationship between Christianity and these disciplines; draw heavily on them for insights which undergird the Christian message and demonstrate the ways in which faith may impact on their teachings and practices.

A THIRST FOR RELEVANCE

4. Tend to view religious faith as irrelevant and other-worldly.

4. Emphasize the Christian faith as something relevant to every aspect of one's life and work, and stress the concerns of today's society rather than a "Sunday-only" or "heavenly-only" type of reality. Use modern translations of Scripture, contemporary Christian writers, and nontraditional religious language in presentations and dialog.[6]

PHILOSOPHICALLY OPEN

5. Are philosophically committed to research, open discussion, and empirical experience as the final validators of truth.

5. Avoid claiming Biblical revelation for something that is only speculation; present Biblical teachings of Christianity as essential tenets that may, however, be explored, investigated, and freely discussed; challenge them to be open to the claims of Christ.

TOLERANT OF DIVERSITY

6. Are more open to diversity of thought and more able to stand outside themselves to see another perspective.

6. Present options for interpretation and alternatives for action rather than fixed answers whenever possible; encourage discussion, dialog, and debate as helpful methods of conversion and growth; be non-defensive and non-threatening.

UNIVERSALISTIC

7. Tend to be universalistic rather than particularistic in their views of religion and salvation.

7. Acknowledge genuine points of congruence between Christianity and other faiths; tactfully point out meaningful differences; stress potential negative impact of the universalist position.

NONAUTHORITARIAN

8. Look to organizations and individuals to establish their authority through competence and moral suasion rather than authoritarian wielding of power or clever manipulation.

8. Deemphasize authoritarian attitudes and styles; convey credibility through calm self-assurance, integrity, genuine compassion, and reliance on the Holy Spirit.

MOTIVATED BY SERVICE NEEDS

9. Tend to act more from esteem, actualization, and service needs than from safety or security needs.

9. Scratch where they itch—present claims of the Gospel addressed to this orientation (e.g., rich young ruler); emphasize the scattering as well as the gathering function of God's people.

SELF-DIRECTED IN LEARNING

10. Are highly self-directed in the process of learning.

10. Involve the educated themselves not only in learning experiences but also in the planning and evaluation of learning; recognize the usefulness and effectiveness of more individualized settings and techniques for learning.

ORIENTED TO VARIETY

11. Prefer diversity and innovation in style and content of programming, services, learning experiences, etc.	11. Offer a variety of programs for the educated tailored to their time schedules, lifestyles, and learning preferences rather than expecting or requiring them to fit into the way "we've always done it."

CRITICAL OF AND IMPATIENT WITH WASTE

12. Less tolerant of boring repetition, senseless get-togethers, and perceived busy work.	12. Quality must be emphasized in all aspects of programming and ministry, particularly in the areas of leadership and resource development; requests for time and talent involvement should relate to meaningful ministry, not routine or counterproductive institutional maintenance.

PREJUDICED AGAINST FAITH

13. May have reservations (or even hostility) about the validity of the Christian faith because their experience of it has been limited to very closed, judgmental, anti-intellectual expressions.	13. Help educated to understand these expressions and the *Sitz im Leben* of those involved in them; lift up true Christianity as broader, intellectually honest, and more humane and liberating than these.

[The above recommendations of Oldham are quite useful. They deal largely with method rather than content. In relating to the educated, however, the Christian should also automatically think of substance, of Law and Gospel, of our potential for greatness as created and redeemed persons. At the same time, the potential for destructiveness because of the Fall infiltrates and threatens to control our mind, will, and emotions, regardless of the level of education or intelligence.

The Christian needs to reinforce these Biblical understandings through personal study of Scripture and application of them in everyday conversation, especially in exchanging views with the educated. Only through daily efforts to think theologically will the Christian acquire the desired expertise to gain rapport with the educated and to present Biblical teachings in their best light. That is the most and the least we can do as we call upon the Holy Spirit to work faith in the hearts of the educated.]

5

Preaching to the Educated

During the "Beatnik" era, I knew a man who attempted a ministry to the Bohemians in San Francisco. He was a warm, personable fellow and showed an intense concern for people. But his ministry never progressed. The reason, he and others felt, was that his approach never went beyond one-on-one and small group relationships to *the proclamation of the Word in a worshiping community*. That just wasn't his style.

But our ministry to the educated is incomplete without a clear proclamation of the Gospel and worship. Nederhood even says the worship service, in which the Word is preached, is *the* most important component in our mission approach to the educated. "No contact with educated people should be judged complete until attendance upon the preaching of the Word results.[1] My ministry as a campus pastor for a dozen years confirmed this—and for several reasons.

For one, you can't be a Christian in a vacuum. Christianity is not a solo experience. I have instructed many university students for church membership who still remained quite at sea until they became an integrated part of a *group* of worshiping Christians.

Further, the educated are particularly attuned to the relevance and import of the verbally communicated Word. Accordingly, the sermon is not intrinsically a "dead duck" as a medium of communication, as some detractors claim.[2]

Third, many educated are drawn to those churches in which the preached Word is embraced within the liturgical heritage of the church—my preference, too. Here the aesthetic sensitivities of the educated and their appreciation for art and music need to be kept in mind.

Accordingly we come back to the educated assembled in a worshiping congregation. What is the message that should be preached?

Nederhood notes three emphases. (1) Since the educated are

inclined to worship the creation rather than the Creator, the doctrine of God's creative activity must be stressed. (2) A decision must be made in confronting the Christ who has come, and who is coming in imminent judgment. (3) The Christian faith has implications for all of life.[3]

Interestingly enough, these three themes comprise the doctrine of the Holy Trinity—and a cogent three-point sermon for preaching to the educated as well.

These topics, but other fundamental concerns as well, need to be examined in considering what is to be preached to the educated.

The Issues in Preaching to the Educated

The Doctrine of Creation vs. the Irrelevance of God. The impact of science upon the educated leads many to affirm a discontinuity between *any* creator and the creation. Many feel that life organized around a faith in God is irrelevant. They say, in effect, "*I* am God."

But they beg the question. When Job cried out to his Maker, "Show me my guilt, O God!" God in essence replied, "Job, you've missed the point. I am the Creator. You are the creature. Where were you when . . . ?" And then comes the whole majestic catalog of creation.[4]

Many of the educated are drinking from a stream the source of which they deny. The Christian points to the God of the universe. It is he who has made us and not we ourselves. As one graduate student appropriately asked his colleague about his research, "Well, what has God been doing in the natural sciences these days?"

God is at work revealing himself in all the orders of creation and society. And this is the God who also revealed himself in the person of his Son. "In fact, every single thing was created through, and for, him."[5]And he alone is to be worshiped in our pursuit of all knowledge and understanding.

Reason: A Good Gift of God. Luther called reason a harlot. But he also spoke of "reason captive under the obedience of faith." *Redeemed reason* is a good gift of God. The disturbing factor for the church "in the intellectual revolt against the Christian faith is the feeling that Christianity means closing the mind—narrowing the vision—while education liberates the mind."[6] The preacher to the educated affirms the gift of the intellect and the joy and duty of glorifying the Giver while humbly, thankfully, and relentlessly pursuing all areas of knowledge.

Guilt. In Albert Camus's *The Fall*,[7] protagonist John Baptiste Clamence subtly shifted the focus from *mea culpa* (my guilt) to *nostra culpa* (our guilt)—"the state of us all." This is the Achilles' heel in many of the characters in literature—and in the lives of many of the educated—and ourselves as well. The educated need to recognize their *personal* accountability and need for repentance before God. Sin is not just that I have hurt the "other" or even myself. It is first and foremost a broken relationship with *God*. "Against thee, thee only have I sinned."[8]

British Rationalist Cyril E. M. Joad, professor of philosophy and religion at the University of London, saw this reality. Rejecting the folly of writing off humanity's "sinfulness" as a mere "by-product of circumstances" he wrote,

> I have come flatly to disbelieve all this. I see now that evil is endemic in man, and that the Christian doctrine of original sin expresses a deep and essential insight into human nature....
>
> Now, of course, it is impossible to adopt such a view in relation to mankind and not to apply it to oneself.... Let me, then, be content to say that the belief in the fundamental, and in this life ineradicable nature of human sinfulness seem to me quite intolerable unless there were some source of guidance and assistance outside ourselves to which we could turn for comfort....
>
> What better hope was offered than by the Christian doctrine that God sent His Son into the world to save the sinners?...
>
> Since it is impossible to live a Christian life alone, let alone to worship God by oneself, the next step was to join a corporate body for Christian worship, to return, in fact, to the bosom of the church, and to set one's feet on the steep and slippery path that leads to heaven.[9]

Joad followed through and became a member of a worshiping community.

Sin only results in our self-imposed isolation from God. But our loving God alone can and has restored the broken relationship and removed our guilt through his Son Jesus Christ our Lord. And so, as the father said to the prodigal son's brother: "We *had* to celebrate and show our joy!"[10]

And let's keep it a celebration. We could err by approaching the educated with harmful preaching that does not appreciate their need for self-respect and self-esteem and that only deepens guilt and reduces the person's potentiality for the kingdom of God. For the educated can easily become all the more proud as a defense reaction to a feeling of inadequacy. As Warren Schmidt states,

> The more a defense is attacked, the more important it becomes to the individual. . . . The real genius of the Christian Gospel . . . is that it *makes pride unnecessary* by assuring men of God's love for sinners.[11]

[Parenthetically, we should note that only Christians can in a true sense say of each other "I'm okay. You're okay." Why? Because true self-respect and self-esteem can only be reached when we first understand God's Law which destroys falsely-based self-respect. Then proper self-esteem as one belonging to God is created by the Gospel. Our concern here is that we *do not become confrontational and belligerent* as we help people realize that all of us are under God's condemnation and as such suffer the greatest possible loss of self-esteem; but we also are given the greatest potential for self-respect, positive development, and greatness when the Spirit works in us through the Gospel.]

Loneliness. Paul Morentz, Lutheran pastor and psychiatrist, once said, "Loneliness is still mankind's greatest problem. And it stems from the 'original sin' of humanity's self-imposed loneliness and isolation from God back in the Garden of Eden."

Loneliness weighs heavily on the educated, too. I find Elizabeth Elliott's Scripturally-based insights most helpful here. She was widowed twice—one husband was martyred in Ecuador; the other died from cancer. She affirms,

1) Be still and know that God is God (Ps. 46).
2) Give thanks—for the promise of God's presence.
3) Refuse self-pity—a death that has no resurrection.
4) Accept your loneliness.
5) Offer up your loneliness to God.
6) Do something for someone else.[12]

But we hasten to add that ultimate loneliness and rejection can only be overcome through Jesus Christ. What a privilege for the preacher to point the educated to the One who says, "I will never leave you, nor forsake you!"[13] His presence is always comforting because Christ's redemptive sacrifice makes it possible for all things to work together for our good.

Organism vs. Organization. Sheldon Vanauken once noted that one of the best arguments against Christianity is the Christians themselves. We are often a poor advertisement for Christianity,[14] and Hale says many people feel they can be "better Christians" outside rather than inside the church.[15]

[It becomes necessary to digress here, because the common and universal mistake made by both Christians and non-Christians is to assume that there is such a person as a *better Christian* or degrees of being *Christian.* The fact is, either we are good, totally Christian or we are not, because we become Christians when through faith we accept the redemption by Jesus Christ and therefore are considered righteous (holy) before God. The common infection of *original* sin remains, to be sure. But even when we Christians commit sins, also those that offend the non-Christian, we are still considered righteous by God if we *confess* our sins to him and in genuine repentance ask for forgiveness. Both Christians and non-Christians will continue to be victims of original sin throughout their earthly life. But the Christian is free, *declared* righteous; so actually there can be no degrees of *better Christians.* Both Christians and non-Christians are wrong when they speak of "better Christians" and when they expect ideal performance from them. (However, one would assume Christians would strive to live more sanctified and socially acceptable lives under Christ and guided by the Scriptures.) All Christians collectively make up *the body of Christ,* often spoken of as *the* church as distinguished from congregations, parishes, and church buildings.]

So the preacher needs to challenge the educated to make a careful distinction between the organization and the organism—between a fallible institution, the mystical body of Christ, and our Lord, its head. Every profession and every corporation, including the organized church, has its foul balls.

What do you do with *him*, all you that pass by? You must contend with *him* who is at the very fulcrum of the universe and all of history. In *him* all things "hang together (1 Col. 1:16)." What will you do then with *him* who is called Christ (Matt. 27:22)?

Choose you this day whom you will serve (Joshua 24:15)!

In sum, we are dealing with two different stumbling blocks. Gilbert Holstein states it well.

> Although in proclaiming God's Word to the educated every care must be taken and every effort made not to place artificial stumbling-blocks in their way (arising from failure to understand the educated), nevertheless the real stumbling-block, the *skandalon* of the cross, far from being minimized or totally omitted, must be accentuated clearly and boldly as God's own power that disturbs, comforts, and transforms those it confronts.[16]

The Gospel Challenge to the True Realization of Self. We can relate to the educated if we realize their need for a sense of self-worth, self-development, and a feeling of accomplishment in making a positive contribution to society.

The Gospel says we are all God's creatures, the crown of his creation. We belong to him and are *worth* much to God. He gave his only Son to die for all people. Therefore we are all called to live creative, service-centered lives for him and for one another. Life in God is the authentic realization of self.[17] For the Holy Spirit works through us, calling us and making us to be the self, the person *God* wants us to be.

Then we can rise above job or occupation to vocation, where everything is seen *sub specie aeternitatis*, in the light of eternity.[18] For the Christian faith has relevance to the totality of life. Christ "fills all things (Eph. 4:10)." Through his body, the church, he is "all in all (Eph. 1:23)." And the true realization of self is seeing everything and doing everything to the glory of God.

> Everything you do or say, then, should be done in the name of the Lord Jesus, as you give thanks through him to God the Father (Col. 3:17).
>
> Whatever you do, work at it with all your heart, as though you were working for the Lord, and not for men (Col. 3:23).

Social Concerns. Although many of the educated, particularly on the university campus, have moved from the social activism of the sixties to the moral relativism, self-absorption and not-the-why-but-the-how of the nineties, social concerns still remain primary in the thinking of many educated adults. In the face of injustice, racism, oppression, and suffering, they feel social change is not only necessary but possible, thinking, if not actually saying, that it is possible to raise the level of society *absolutely*.

The preacher is called to address these issues. Our Lord's approach to the individual and society was holistic, and ours must be, too. He not only forgave a man's sins, but healed him as well.

Preaching to social issues—and being involved in "pouring oneself out" (Philippians 2) for humanity—is no mere matter of "politics from the pulpit." Biblical preaching will address compartmentalized lives that see spirituality as alien to our social encounters and the way people are oppressed by some institutions.

Sharon Streater says "the world is out there crying for life, seeking for justice, craving for food, wishing that there were a reason to hope."[19] The church must "be real to life, taking its responsibility of being a prophetic voice and a self-denying servant seriously."[20]

The church needs to reflect the God who established it, the God of justice, of liberation, and of committed love. The church must be involved in bringing justice, liberation, and love to the world in which it exists, not a sentimental emotionalism, but a self-denying, sacrificial giving to the lives of others. This is what spirituality is all about.[21]

So, in reaching to others we are reached, in giving we receive, in changing we are changed, in transforming we are transformed. As a church called to serve we must continue to seek out and communicate with those whom we are here to serve. The church is the servant of all to whom Christ came to reveal the love of God, the whole of humanity. This means even those who are our critics and who seem to have energy and a motivation that we ourselves sometimes lack. This also means that at times we are to humble ourselves and learn from those whom we may not even consider part of us. We are one humanity, equally created in the image of God, and, more important, redeemed from our fallenness by Christ. Therefore we can learn and grow from the knowledge of all persons who share with us. God is one; truth is one; truth is universal. Our task is to believe and trust God and his promises and to manifest our faith in love for others.

> Christ in us is the mystery and the hope of eternity. It is a reality to humbly realize and to joyfully share. As was said, "they will know you are Christians by your love," not by your words that are not fulfilled in love.[22]

Death. It is naive to think all the educated fear death. I know surgeons who face it daily and do not fear it. I knew a lieutenant colonel who served with the marines in Bouganville who said if there was anything beyond the grave he would take his punishment like a man.

A book publisher in Berkeley proudly told me his death would be like his father's—"no more than just a light bulb going out." A theological professor who lost his faith said he didn't know about life after death, but whatever happened, he would just "give up his life as sort of an offering."

But they may be atypical. Other educated adults struggle with the ultimate meaninglessness and futility of their existence.[23] They see the inevitability of death, even though they may wish, as William Saroyan said, "In my case, I think they should make an exception." They may exude pessimism or even foreboding and grave concern for the nuclear holocaust to come—and any part they have had in precipitating it.

The preacher must address this universal. The proclaimer of the Good News points to the One who conquered death and "brought life and immortality to light through the Gospel (2 Cor. 1:10)." The communicator of the Gospel preaches as a dying person to a dying humanity, but does so with the sure and certain hope that "in Christ all shall be made alive (1 Cor. 15:22)" and that in him "we have passed from death to life (1 John 3:14)," for our Lord has said,

> Because I live, you will live also (1 John 3:14).
> Whoever lives and believes in me shall never die (John 11:26).

These are some of the issues to be addressed in preaching to the educated. But what is the heart of the theology to be preached?

The Message to be Preached

What is *primary* in our preaching of the Good News, the Gospel? Is it *love*?

I submit that love is important but penultimate. From beginning to end, the prophets' message was *repent,* and our Lord's final, climactic words to his disciples (Luke 24:46–49) were that "the message about repentance *to* the forgiveness of sins . . . must be preached to all nations." Note that *repentance to* (leading to; Gk., *eis*) is the preferable reading, not *repentance and*. The preaching of the Law is to bring about conviction of sin and the reception of the Good News of the Gospel.

For Luke, repentance equals conversion. "Repentance to (*eis*) means "resulting in," "with a view to" the forgiveness of sins. Not that repentance *causes* salvation, but that conversion takes place *so that* people receive God's forgiveness. Luke stresses *all* nations.[24]

This is also the message which is essential to Paul's declaration of the Gospel (see 1 Corinthians 15; 2 Corinthians 5), and it is the central core of the sermons in the book of Acts. (Study Acts 2:38; 3:15; 3:19–20; 13:38–39; 15:9, etc.) Repentance *to* the forgiveness of sins is always the heart of the declaration—and note how it is linked to the resurrection.

The life of sanctification follows, of course, and will be preached upon.[25] But the "glowing core," as Einar Billing says, is the Gospel of the forgiveness of sins.

> Anyone wishing to study Luther would indeed be in peril of going astray were he not to follow this rule: never believe that you have a correct understanding of a thought of Luther before you have succeeded in reducing it to a simple corollary of the thought of the *forgiveness of sins*.[26]

This is our message and our task when preaching to the educated adult.[27]

6

The Educated and the Bible

Edward A. Rauff in *Why People Join the Church* noted that the key reason was "friends and relatives." Typical of this is the experience of a burgeoning parish, so vibrant in their fellowship that a third Sunday morning service was added to accomodate their worshippers. What is significant is that the church appeals to young adults, and even more important, also to single adults. In response to queries, newcomers reported that they were primarily attracted to the parish by the genuineness and openness of relationships and the friendliness and warmth of the people and pastors.[1] Such a spirit of genuine warmth and openness is the perfect channel for achieving the crucial goal of getting the educated into the Holy Scriptures.

Several student papers on this topic stood out in the course Reaching the Educated Adult. Jan Smith Wood wrote on "Putting Bible Study in Perspective." Seeing the Scriptures as icon rather than idol, this Episcopal laywoman and seminary graduate proposed lay-led, small-group Bible study in parishioners' homes.

The problem came into sharp focus as Wood asked people what *they* wanted to learn in a summer program. Almost unanimously they responded: "I don't know anything about the Bible—not even enough to tell you what I want to learn."

Quoting Roland Seboldt that the goal for parish education for adults is not knowledge, but faith,[2] Wood stated the objectives of her summer course.

> To enable people to carry on small group Bible study; to claim Holy Scripture as crucial to our own faith journeys; to allow Scripture to impact our daily living as both relevant and revelant.
>
> Perhaps the imagery that most fits my understanding of the role and purpose of Christian Education is that of a caged bird

that is lifted up, set free, and soars into the air. It already knows how to fly—it just needs to be lifted up and let loose! . . .

The Church has a special responsibility to teach. In this, we must always remember that we are not teaching religion, rather we are teaching people. The focus of Christian Education must always be the people, both in community and as individuals. To teach people rather than religion means that education is always dynamic, and all-inclusive of every part of our faith-filled lives. The role of educator must be to "lead out," to help others uncover that which they already own as children of God in Christ, and as members of the Christian community. Furthermore, every educator must be ever mindful that to be educator, one must also be student. True learning is not a matter of "open brain, insert information." It is a question of dialog and genuine conversation.

We will only become paralyzed when we forget that the real work is done by the Word of God. The real work is done by the Word of God Incarnate: in living relationship with Christ. The real work is done by the Word of God active in every generation through the Holy Spirit. The real work is done by the Word of God in Holy Scripture and in our daily lives as they, too, are Holy Scripture. Finally the real work is done by the Word of God met in the very words of Christian doctrine.

It is my fervent hope that upon the close of the summer, the participants will form their own small groups within which they will continue to wrestle with their understanding of Holy Scripture and its pertinence to their daily lives. Like Jacob wrestling with the angel, we are called to engage God in the here and now. One way we may do this is through active attendance to the Word of God which is made present to us through the Bible.[3]

Another student, Robert A. Atwood, analyzed the approaches used in the Scriptures for preaching, teaching, and reaching out to the educated adult. Especially intriguing was his analysis of the sermons in the book of Acts—the sermon, its content, the result of the preached message, and the motivation that presumably was used.

Atwood's judgment was that

The technique used most by Christ was that of getting his hearer to draw his own final conclusion, to do some thinking on his own. This he did through questions that he did not directly answer, through answers that led to further thinking, and in at least one case through complimenting the hearer on his answer

> to Christ's question. This technique is used by Paul in his epistles, though Paul usually gives the answer. Christ was also not afraid to challenge the hearer to action of some sort as proof of learning.[4]

Atwood also noted the many variations of the *kerygma* used by New Testament preachers and how they sought to vary their preaching to fit the different types they met. Both Christ and Paul used contemporary illustrations.

William Diehl's discussion of house churches and Christian support groups in *Christianity and Real Life* is germane to our subject. The participants themselves must form the relationships. It's not a "count-off" process like choosing teams for softball. Also the learners are the educators; they decide the shape of their study. It may be issues of contemporary concern (global, communal, familial) but seen in the light of Holy Writ. They may grapple with questions raised by Scripture itself and how these issues impact on daily living. "They may determine group affiliation based upon profession, or area of residence, or affinity, or subject of interest.[5]

These principles, the *preeminence of Bible-study* and *participant-generated* group formation and focus[6] are the clues to getting adults, particularly educated adults, into "the atomosphere in which grace flourishes,"[7] the worshiping community.[8]

Many an outreach has failed because an individual was invited to a Bible Class at a strange church, and perhaps came a long distance, but then the person fell away because the inviter had "built a long complex bridge with many toll gates to go through."

What is needed is "natural bridge building," such as small Bible study groups in members' homes.

A true missionary at heart was the Rev. Arthur Haake who "died in the saddle" in the fifties while serving as pastor of West Portal Lutheran Church, San Francisco. He would call on people whose names had been given him by his members—FBI men, attorneys, physicians. He visited with these people, but never stressed "joining the church." Nor did he slip his parish bulletin under a Playboy magazine before he left. They would simply chat, and he would ask if they wished him to come back again. After several meetings he would say, "Oh, by the way, you've completed about half of my adult inquiry class. I wonder if you'd like to join with some other people who are doing the same thing?" Often people did—and eventually became members of his parish.[9]

A parish in Annapolis, Maryland, started a second church which began still another. And the mother church has now started two more churches within a sixty-mile radius. Their formula was Bible study and more Bible study.[10] Much prayer goes into their selection of Bible study elders/leaders and of the seed couples/singles which form groups that meet for ten weeks. At the end of that period the selection process begins again and new groups are formed. *Divide and multiply* is the principle.

The pastor only drops in briefly during the course to encourage. This offsets the impression of just wanting to get more members for the organized church. Lay-led and lay-oriented, such a setting is particularly inviting and appealing to the educated who, as we have seen, have the capacity for creativity, fresh learning, and self-generated leadership.

By the end of the session, a new couple has six to eight new friends all from the same church. There is now a natural bridge to the greater worshiping community, the pastor's adult class, and later advanced Bible study groups. A dentist summed up his experience:

> At first I resisted the Lamplighters and had no interest in the program being offered. Then an M.D. friend of mine invited me to a study at his house and I went because of friendship. What I found, however, was a giving, sharing type love that was so real and beautiful. Over the weeks of our study a real excitement developed in the class. By the time our class was over I was so excited that I started my own class, and under the blessing of the Holy Spirit the same love and excitement has permeated this group. The Lamplighter Bible Study can provide an inner strength and an outreach into the community for any church that will use the program.[11]
>
> In these and similar ways we can invite the educated into the Holy Scriptures. There, as they experience the "faith which was once delivered unto the saints" (Jude 3) and are surrounded by "so great a cloud of witnesses" (Heb. 12:1) of Biblical history, they can for themselves feel the brush of angels' wings as they meet our Lord himself in his sacred Word.[12]

7

The Case Study

The case study method is invaluable for helping the educated to think theologically. After using the case below, one woman followed me one hundred feet out of the church asking, "What happened to Harriet?"

However, the purpose in analyzing a case is not to give the answer but to practice skills of sound reasoning and to assess the completeness of the study.

Business and law professors from Harvard University taught the class I took at the Case Study Institute in the summer of 1974. They insisted that the teacher keep an extremely neutral role. During the intense, fifty-minute sessions the teachers probed, baited, and challenged us with the concluding dilemma of the case: 1) what would *you* do? and 2) *why* would you do it?

The characters in the case are minutely studied, the issues clarified, and the consequences of possible decisions are weighed. It is crucial to deal only with the given facts and not indulge in reminiscences or go off on other tangents.

It is vital that students prepare by reading the case very critically, indeed, as if reading a detective story, looking for hidden clues.

The theological advantages in using the case method are many. It is a most helpful tool for pastors and laity together tackling the ethical issues of our day that deal with Christianity and life. Although the following case does not deal strictly with "the world of the educated," it does demonstrate that this exciting method of learning can enrich the lives of the educated as one more approach in creative inquiry.

We Just Can't Go on Meeting like This![1]

"I still can't believe it," said Harry Ransome. "Our pastor, Ashby Dean Atkinson III, with an illegitimate child for 17 years. Incredible!"

The little group of parishioners, dumb with grief, like mourners edging away from a casket, nodded in agreement.

"And what will he do now," asked aging Suzie Schlaegel, "stay or leave? And—what do *we* do?"

The Church with the Red Doors

It was May 15, 1974. A congregational meeting had just been held that evening at Blessed Sacraments Church in Duncan, Texas—the "church with the red doors" as it was affectionately known in the neighborhood. The parish of 200 members was well-knit, with mostly younger couples and many children.

Pastor Ashby Dean Atkinson III had been there ten years. After seminary and five years in a semi-rural parish, he had come to Blessed Sacraments. A graduate of Eastern Seminary, he was well known for his powerful preaching. There was also a vigorous Christian education program and mission outreach into the community. Only one thing marred the scene. Many people commented that something must be wrong between the pastor and his wife, although nothing had ever really surfaced.

The pastor was often praised by his parishioners. But when it happened in his wife's presence, she frequently would say something like, "Well, it's nice you feel that way. But you don't know him like I know him." And sometimes she would add, "If you only knew."

Forgiven and Forgotten?

Pastor Atkinson had met his wife during seminary days. During their long engagement, she became pregnant. At that time, seminary rules forbade marriage before graduation. So with pressure from both their parents, they decided to put the child up for adoption when the baby was born. Only the dean of the seminary and a limited number of relatives knew of the birth and adoption. Atkinson graduated and accepted his first parish. Atkinson and his wife were married during the summer following completion of seminary training.

As the years passed, Atkinson's ministry prospered, but his wife kept before him the memory of their first child. More than once Atkinson told his wife, "Harriet, I've asked God to forgive me—to forgive us for having a child out of wedlock, and he has. I hold no ill will against you. I hope you hold none against me. Why can't you accept the fact that we were wrong? Why can't you accept God's forgiveness—and accept yourself in the bargain? Thank God for his forgiveness through Jesus Christ. Now may I only share it with my people."

As the years passed, Atkinson's ministry prospered—especially since his coming to Blessed Sacraments. But as Harriet Atkinson approached menopause, she increasingly threatened Atkinson with exposure. Contrarily, at one point she planned self-committal at a nearby mental hospital. But the morning a friend was going to drive her there, Harriet cancelled the trip saying, "But I can't leave the children." At that point they had three, ages 14, 12, and 9.

In early May of 1974 things came to a head. Harriet called the president of the congregation, insisting on a congregational meeting. Harry Ransome, the president, said, "But why, exactly?"

"You need to know the truth about this man.... There's a problem that—uh—well, I *have* forgiven my husband. But well—uh—well, the parish has just got to know. That's what forgiveness is all about. We've been living a lie in front of you, but we owe it to you to let you know the truth." And she hung up the receiver.

Ransome met with Pastor and Mrs. Atkinson a few hours later and asked for more information. Both filled him in on the background of their problem, but then Ransome pressed the question again as to why a full congregation meeting had to be held.

""Well, Harry," said Atkinson, "I thought Harriet and I had this resolved between us but I guess it isn't. Maybe it will never be until everybody knows about it."

Harriet added: "Harry, I love the Lord, I love this church, and I love this man. And I don't want to destroy his ministry. I mean to *help* it. Here's a chance for all of us to know what real forgiveness is all about. I can't go on and I can't see Ashby going on—living a lie—it's hypocrisy—it's...."

Atkinson interrupted, "I don't think it's hypocrisy but I can't live with this pressure and knowing the agony you're going through, Harriet. I feel God's forgiveness. I'm sorry you don't. If bringing this out in the open will help you, I'll go through with it, no matter what the cost. I hope people will understand. It was a long time ago...."

Ransome replied, "But isn't there another way? Perhaps in time. . . ."

But Harriet countered, "Seventeen years, Harry, I can't take it any more. Call the meeting or I'll call the judicatory president."

Later that week Ransome set the meeting for May 15. At the meeting, to which only those over age 18 were invited, Ransome explained the history behind the Atkinsons' problem, and let the pastor take the floor. Atkinson's comments were brief. He said he was sorry the parish had to suffer through his and his wife's personal problems this way, assured them he felt God's forgiveness, asked for theirs, and sat down.

Ransome arose and turned towards Mrs. Atkinson. "I really don't know what to say next," he began.

Harriet stood up and shaking openly, said, "I'm sorry, too, that this had to come out this way. But you had to know. It was a child of love—and I love the Lord, and I love my husband—and I love the ministry. But I feel in my heart—close as we all are here—that you needed to know us as we really are—and forgive us. *I* need to know that."

As Mrs. Atkinson sat down, several members asked for the floor, generally commending Atkinson and his wife for their ministry to them. Then, as emotions mounted, with many people crying openly, Ransome asked for order. As the room quieted down, he said, "The main thing, Pastor and Mrs. Atkinson, is that we meet as fellow sinners here tonight. And we want you to know, Pastor, that we *understand*. We forgive you—both of you—as God has forgiven us. We love you both and you, sir, are our pastor!"

After the members left the church and approached their cars, some in crushed silence, others agitatedly talking, a variety of views were expressed.

Jim Detman said: "I've never heard a man preach forgiveness as he does, in any parish I've ever worshiped in. He's experienced it. He should stay."

Jasmine Clark said, "Believe me, I'm faithful to my husband, but I do admire that man Atkinson! What hell he has had to live through! I, too, think he should stay. I sure don't feel like throwing rocks tonight."

Elizabeth Betts said: "Yes, but talk about hell, think of what Harriet has been through. It was her baby. Think of *her* guilt and pain—over the years. A man can throw himself into his work. But a woman—you know, it took real courage for her to do what she did tonight. Now I really wonder about Atkinson all these years!"

Old Gus Kraszholtz commented, "The question is, can *we* as a parish, and as individuals, really forgive—and live that forgiveness? Not that God won't give the grace, but will we *practice* it in the months and years ahead?"

Curt Adams said, "I love this guy, too, but frankly, I just can't see his effectiveness at Blessed Sacraments after tonight. And think of the effect on our children."

Harold Hansen smashed his fist in his hand and said, "I think he should commit his wife to a hospital, and stay! *She's* the problem!"

Bill Duncan said, "I just can't absorb all this at once. I think we—some group in the parish—should meet again to learn more."

But graying Suzie Schlaegel said, "This is too traumatic to happen to *any* congregation more than once. I hope the problem was resolved tonight with your closing statement, Harry. Now let the principals work it out—not the whole congregation. We just can't go on meeting like this."

Like every case, the above becomes a springboard for discussion, specifically for theological exploration of a practical problem. The direction of the exchange will vary each time. In some manner the analysis should touch upon these topics: human nature; perfect creation followed by the Fall; redemption by Jesus Christ, but considered against the residue of sinful tendencies that remain with everyone; forgiveness by God; forgiveness by Christians; the implications and practical applications of forgiveness for life; the pastor and his office and person as distinguished from other Christians; clarification of the distorted, common belief that there can be a better *Christian;* and possibilities for growth in Christian living. An imaginative and creative analysis of a case such as this can lead naturally and without embarrassment to interesting and gainful theological discussion with the educated.

8
Building Trust with the Educated

What follows is the substance of a concluding lecture in the course Reaching the Educated Adult. I emphasized cultivating a trust-relationship with the educated—in and outside the church, using the following sequence of topics:

—the attitude when approaching the educated,
—barriers and bridges in communication,
—the dynamics of the one-to-one relationship,
—discouraging imitation of self, and
—catching God's vision of the "other."

Attitude and Evangelization

A natural and informal approach to the educated was stressed. By contrast, much of the material on evangelization is *intentional,* dealing with *strategy, programs,* and *boldness* in witnessing. I quite agree, boldness is required. I even wrote a book, *Bold Ones on Campus: A Call for Christian Commitment.*[1] "We cannot but speak the things which we have seen and heard" (Acts 4:20.29) And we speak with authority (not authoritarianism), because we are representatives of an authority, "the author and perfecter of our faith" (Heb. 12:2). We dare not lose our boldness as we witness for Christ. We need to be deeply committed to sharing the Gospel with people—and it should show. But many—particularly the educated—will be turned off by a misplaced or ill-timed boldness. There is also a time to be *intentional* about our relaxedness.

The answer lies in a balance, a way of thinking about evangelization, that takes into account the following:

1. The individual personality of the witness.

Each person has been given particular abilities and limitations for witnessing.[2] Sometimes initial shyness in sharing the Gospel must be overcome by just beginning in your own "stumbling, fumbling way." These were the words of a lay person who decided to leave the "secret service" and the company of those described in Mark 16:8 who "said nothing to anyone, because they were afraid." The Spirit-given gift of witnessing may be waiting to be tapped—that ability to simply say "This is 'What Jesus Means to Me.' "[3] (Remember the man who was in prison for thirty years, but one day tried the door and found it unlocked.)

2. The individual personality of the person to whom one witnesses.

How close is this person to the kingdom of God? Considering this person's specific character and needs, what is the best way to communicate the Gospel?[4] In other words, how can this unique person best be reached?

The term *evangelism* is offensive to some; TV evangelists sometimes annoy; and previous encounters with offensive or inept witnesses to Christ may have made them wary. We need to be keenly sensitive to people's understandable suspicion and resistance.

3. The best setting for witness.

Choosing the time for dialog is crucial.[5] What are the circumstances? What approach is best at the moment? Is this the time for direct confrontation? Is more time needed for building trust? Is it better to wait for a more appropriate setting to speak the Gospel specifically? Trust is vital if the person is to be receptive. "To everything there is a season" (Eccl. 3:1).

So for effective witness it is necessary to balance the setting and the timing and develop a trust between the witness and the other person. The witness is there to listen and to learn from the other, to respond to the needs of the other, and to choose the particular aspects of the Gospel that need to be stressed at the time.

One setting may call for just listening. Another, for just sharing your own faith in a relaxed manner, without any "call for decision." Then again the time will come for a more direct challenge to deal with who Christ is and what he did—and his claims on each of us.

In summary, I believe the witness needs to be perceptive about the dimensions of the moment and know which tack (not *strategy*) to take. This attitude is both relaxed *and* intentional, informal *and* bold, patient *and* persistent. That is the only way to witness.

That is the tone of Harry A. DeWire's book *The Christian as Communicator*:

> [The Christian] shows that witnessing consists of speech, most certainly, but it also consists of many other things, including silence. There is no formula for all occasions, no pattern to apply, no bag of tricks. Above all overt acts and words, the Christian's primary witness, is in being a Christian. What he is speaks louder than anything he can say. When something more is needed, the nature of that something will appear. In every case he may be quite relaxed, knowing that his responsibility ends with providing the occasion for the result—the result itself being in God's hands alone through the operation of his Holy Spirit in the minds and hearts of men.[6]

Barriers and Bridges

Some of the many barriers to communication of the Gospel should be repeated here: the institutional church's take-over of the individual's responsibility for witness; the "under and separate" role of the laity (cf. Diehl); the ghetto-like nature of many congregations; and the fact that many Christians are either tongue-tied or untrained.[7]

The beginning point is Christians' rediscovery of their "apostolate by fact"[8] or finding their actual spiritual gifts. Haven't you seen this wonderful process in action?

A pastor in St. Louis told me there was a person in his parish who always shied away from committees or any office in the church. But he was always doing a multitude of individual services around the church. The pastor called him his *saint.*

At University Lutheran Chapel in Berkeley during the fifties we had a weekly student supper hour at which time we lined up pairs of students to make calls on those who had signed a Lutheran preference on their registration cards at the university.[9] I still remember one quiet, soft-spoken young man who went around the group each Sunday night with a clipboard asking others, "Which night could you make some calls?" That one person did more in promoting evangelism during the school year than any committee ever did.

A hospital chaplain told me of a woman to whom he was ministering who was totally paralyzed. She was 37 years old, had three children at home, but now was lying in a $3,000 bed which moved up and down to assist her breathing. There she lay—day and night. "I always hoped," the chaplain said, "that she wouldn't ask me, 'Pastor, what's my purpose in life?' And then one day I stopped outside her room. The door was only slightly open, and I could see another patient sitting there in her wheelchair, very depressed. And the woman lay on the bed, talking to her, saying (as the bed pulsed up and down), 'Keep your chin up, Sue! Never say die!' And in an instant I had the answer to her question."

What one individual can do!

In addition the language I use in dialog with others needs intensive, periodic re-examination. Warren Schmidt reminds us of the six messages involved in communication:

—what you *mean* to say;

—what you *actually* say;

—what the other person *hears;*

—what the other person *thinks* he hears;

—what the other person *says*; and

—what you *think* the other person hears.[10]

I "rediscovered the wheel" on this one once when asked to speak to a group in Illinois. The person who called me was a college coed; so as the days rushed by, the audience I had in mind was college students. I raced my car down the highway that Sunday afternoon, past the cornfields, arriving the very moment I was to speak. I walked through the country church door and was "on."

The church was filled with about one hundred youth, tightly packed in the pews. They had already been sitting there in that hot, stuffy church for an hour or more. I began my presentation on the characters in which we see ourselves in modern novels and dramas.

"How many of you have read *Catcher in the Rye*?" I asked brightly. I got the Great Stone Face. "*Death of a Salesman*?" All the students back in St. Louis knew these books well. But this was not St. Louis, and my audience was high school youth from the farms, not college students. I will not detail my agony as to how I quickly sought to recast my material. But in a word, I fell flat on my face. At least I felt I did. Though the pastor afterward said it wasn't all that bad—that I eventually got through to them, I had learned a lesson: know your audience. Know the thought world and language level of the person with whom you wish to dialog.

A seminary student recounts a similar experience. He was urging a first grade parochial school class, "Elucidate! Elucidate!" They stared up at him blankly. He decided to really come down to their level: "Elaborate! Elaborate!" But they still stared at him. Later the supervising teacher handed him a list of fifteen words he had used in his lesson plan which the students had never heard before.

Communication takes place when you transmit a message to another person, that person understands it, has the *Aha!* experience, and sends a message back—maybe even shaking his fist under your chin at the church door after hearing a sermon he didn't like. That's communication!

Beyond that, we must sanctify our methods of communication. "The means must be as Christian as the ends" (O. H. Theiss). The craft and the message must go in the same direction.

I once had a clever idea for giving my parishioners "prescriptions" when I made my pastoral calls. I had the forms printed up and carried the pads with me.

SPIRITUAL PRESCRIPTION FORM

REV. DON DEFFNER, M.A., B.D.

UNIVERSITY LUTHERAN CHAPEL

2740 College Avenue • Berkeley 5, California

For____________________ Date__________

℞ Address____________________

Take this to:

THE HOLY BIBLE

Take Daily as Directed

Search Well Before Using

Don't Accept Any Substitute ____________________ I.N.J.

I used them for some time, but then one day a sophisticated graduate student told me, "You know, that little gimmick of yours turned me off on you for about six months."[11] I never used the "spiritual prescription forms" again.

There were some positive responses to the little form. A 30-year old woman dying of cancer kept them in her Bible by her bed.

The question is one of *timing*. Considering this person's needs, what particular approach is best? That requires

—taking a fresh look at your personal calling to witness,

—fulfilling your responsibility to convey meaning clearly, and

—checking the sanctification and appropriateness of your methods.

Because everything done communicates (for good or ill), the Christian's task is to be one's self—a nurturing, edifying, burden-bearing child of God.[12]

> There is some question as to whether our planned, purposive encounters as communicators accomplish as much as the simple and natural act of "living among" others. Much time should be spent asking what one needs to say and be *in life* as well as *in the incidents of life*.[13]

The Dynamics of Encounter

"Be what you are." And when you have lived and walked daily in the Word of God in the Scriptures, when you are prayerfully prepared, know that the Holy Spirit is with you in your witnessing. *You are not alone*.

> There is probably a great deal of truth in the fact that we would be a lot less concerned about *how* we approach people if our lives were in true perspective. There is good Scriptural support (Matt. 10:19) for the assumption that if a person has a firm Christian grounding in his own life, he will automatically know what to say and when to say it.[14]

The Matt. 10:19 passage is a particularly powerful comfort for the shy or fearful witness: "When they deliver you up, do not be anxious how you are to speak or what to say; for what you are to say will be given to you in that hour." The 1973 *RSV Common Bible* translates it, "This will be a time for you to bear testimony. Settle it therefore in your minds, not to meditate beforehand how to answer; for I will give you a mouth and wisdom, which none of your adversaries will be able to withstand or contradict."

This latter paraphrase, "not to meditate beforehand" is also an apt reminder of the dangers in following lockstep methodologies of evangelization.[15] We need preparation, yes, but flexibility as well, and an ongoing sensitivity to the fact that others may not be where we think they are, or going where we'd like them to go.[16]

That means start with *active listening*. This is the very first recommendation for the church in Hale's study.[17] The abundant literature on developing this skill need not be rehearsed in detail here.[18] In brief, there is only one justifiable way that the Christian can come into the presence of other people. He will learn how to listen and listen completely.[19]

Carl Rogers's classic response is apropos at this point: "Hmmm . . . hmmm . . . hmmm. . . ." Nor should one jump in too quickly and say, "I understand!" The other person may well feel you don't understand at all! Indeed, we can never fully understand *their* pain, *their* frustrations, *their* doubts. But we can listen sensitively, and this skill needs development.[20]

> The "professing" Christian is a "professional." He works hard at the thing he is supposed to do, whether he feels like it or not.[21]
>
> One of the best definitions of a professional is "a person who can do a good job when he doesn't feel like it." He has learned his stuff. That definition fits the surgeon who can see twenty people in the office in the morning and then do five operations in the afternoon. When the fifth operation comes up at five thirty, does such a surgeon say with glee: "Goody, goody! Time for one more before dinner?" Not if he is in his right mind! He merely does it. And does it well. That surgeon is a professional.[22]

I have a large poster in my study that has an empty balloon over the words, *It often shows a fine command of language to say nothing.*

A pastor was on his way home from the funeral of his dearest friend, a man who had died suddenly in his thirties. He was in O'Hare Airport, feeling very dejected. He wanted to talk to no one. A group of young evangelists began badgering him with questions about what he believed, was he saved, and so on. When he failed to respond with the phrases they wanted, they said in exasperation, "Oh, you pagan businessmen are all alike!" To which he quietly replied, "Look, you don't even know where I'm at—what I'm going through. I am a Christian. And you—you may love your Jesus, but it's certain you don't love me."[23]

The skills of listening and of silence also involve the earlier-noted element of *timing*. That means not just sensing the ***kairos***, the fitting moment for the fitting word, but the time people need to feel sure trust has been established and they can safely open up on what is most intimate to them.[24]

A young woman once came into my office and began complaining about the choir and the Lutheran liturgy, which was still unfamiliar to her, a recent convert. We talked for an hour, and I did what I thought was fairly good counseling. But finally the little red light went on in the back of my brain. I decided to be quiet for a while and listen.

The silence was intolerable for me. There was the relentless feeling to want to jump in and say something. But I just sat there, without a word. After about three minutes which seemed like three hours, she finally spoke. "You know, Pastor," she said, "I guess I should tell you why I really came in to see you. I've been sleeping with my fiancee and I just *had* to talk to you about it."

And then the real counseling began.

Time. Listening. Patience. It may take months to establish a deep trust-relationship with some people.

"The best place for us to witness is among those with whom we have the deepest relationship. Only then can love do its work."[25]

I once had a friend who was a brilliant, caustic, anti-Christian agnostic graduate student at the University of California in Berkeley. It took a whole year to develop a trust-relationship with him.[26] Another relationship has been developing for a generation, but my friend still says, "Don, I just can't see it. What you say about that little Jew hanging on a cross 2000 years ago—it just doesn't make sense. If some of the greatest philosophical minds of history haven't come up with the answers, how can I?" But our trust relationship (and our dialog) continues.

Joost A. M. Merloo once wrote,

> Would you convince your opponent? Then touch his heart—if he has one. One cannot conquer anyone's belief with words and arguments. He merely adjusts them to his own truths and prejudices—unless he likes you.[27]

I would change the word *opponent* to *friend,* acknowledge he has a heart, and replace *likes you* with *trusts you.* But Merloo's insight on the inadequacy of *argument* is very perceptive. In my generation-long friendship cited above never once has there been a heated religious debate, anger, or a cross word. The deep friendship continues. And I continue to listen. However, I also avoid the mistake of thinking more highly of myself than I ought to when I listen but do not speak.

Among professionals a subtle assumption is that they are somehow superior to those who speak, rather than listen, and that the good counselor always does well when he is listening, but not so well when he is speaking.[28]

The speaking must ultimately come, but the listening must also have served its purpose. People don't usually become Christians just because they have seen high moral character in someone.[29] The *verba*—the words about who Christ was and what he did *for us*—must ultimately be shared. And the Holy Spirit will provide the moment—and the very words—for the Good News about Jesus and the resurrection.[30]

But during those days, weeks, months, or years of trust-building the non-Christian should see the *mind of Christ* in the Christian. Even in the face of the doubter's rejection of Christ, *compassion* should always be evident. I am repeatedly struck by one simple line in the gospel of Mark. A man has turned away from our Lord; we can just see his turned back receding into the distance; and the gospel records a profound comment about our Lord at the meeting: "And he, beholding him, loved him."[31]

Even in the face of rejection, Christ's love—and ours—is constant.

This patient, continued *acceptance-of-the-unaccepting* can lead to further dialog. The Christian cares.

> [The non-Christian] finds himself seeking out the Christian because the event of their being together is not simply the construction of agreed-upon barricades from behind which they will hurl their own ego-gratifying ammunition, but rather, a table spread for an event of Christian love.[32]

A friend of mine, a surgeon, came to my home late one Sunday evening, and said, "Hi. Whatcha doin'?" I said, "Nothing, come on in." Actually I had been glued to my first new color TV set, but my friend had come.

He explained the grueling weekend he had had. An eight year-old girl had just died a few hours before, and he was emotionally exhausted. He told how after her death he came out into the hall and told the sad news to the girl's parents. "We did everything we could for her," he said. "But she's gone. I'm very sorry."

"But at that point," the surgeon told me, "the woman turned to her husband and said, 'Well, Louis, it's the will of God. Let's go home.' "

"Don, what's that *will of God* crap all about?" He continued to pour out his exhaustion and frustration at what the woman had said. I tried to explain as best I could that I didn't agree with the woman that God really willed death for us, but that we brought death upon ourselves through the fall into sin, and the *time* of our death in the final analysis is in God's hands. We just talked calmly for a while. I didn't see this as a time to "move in for the kill." My friend wanted to talk to me. He knew he wouldn't get a theological broadside. He trusted me.[33]

I once read that Bonhoeffer shared his cell with an atheist. One night the bombing was particularly intense, and the "atheist" became terrified. But all Bonhoeffer said to him at that point was, "I think it'll be over in about ten minutes." For Bonhoeffer that was proper timing. Another might have considered it the ideal time to witness.

How inappropriate it would have been for our Lord on the cross to hand out tracts to the right and the left! Even the thought of it is offensive.

Imitatio Christi Non Mei

Of special concern during this unhurried self-examination is that the other person not model him- or herself after the particular personality of the Christian—working on an *imitatio mei* rather than an *imitatio Christi*, to use the phrase of Thomas à Kempis.

> The Christian is not eager to "create" another in his own image. He sets an example, not of what the other one can become if he tries hard enough, but of full trust that where two or three meet in the name of Christ, something can happen to the lives of all participants.[34]

God calls us to be what *he* wants us to be.[35] Peter A. Bertocci beautifully captures that concept. I handed out literally thousands of "What Makes a Christian Home?" in which Bertocci actually is speaking of the love of one marital partner for another, but the comparison of the Christian's love for the non-Christian in dialog is valid and beautiful. Bertocci says God is the Third Partner. The vision of the other person and of the relationship is never centered in either partner. I love the *other* so that the other finds new depths and ranges to his/her being. The individual is to grow to the fullness of the nature God allows. Then comes the clincher: *I am to catch God's vision of him/her.*[36]

That attitude can radically improve a marriage. "Love . . . serves no utilitarian purpose. In a sense, love must be useless to be genuine."[37] That attitude prevents an *imitatio mei* from occurring, frees the neophyte to become one's own Christian person, and aids the other in promoting God's vision of who that individual can become.[38]

> We must love those we seek to save, but we must love Christ more; we must love them because we love Christ, because he loves them, because he gave himself for them. We must strive to win souls, not for ourselves, but for Christ. It is not enough to get people to love us; we must get them to love our Savior, to trust in him, and to commit their lives to him. We must hide ourselves away out of sight. He who is thinking of his own honor as he engages in any Christian service is not a vessel ready to be used by Christ. We need to take care that no shadows of ourselves, of our pride, our ambition, our self-seeking, fall upon our work for Christ.[39]

We need to release the other person from every attempt on our part to regulate, coerce, or dominate the individual with our love.[40] The other person needs independence of us, and the time comes when we should say, "And now I leave you to Christ and his Word! You're on your own! The Holy Spirit will be with you!"

Having met the other person with the clear Word of God we now must, in Bonhoeffer's words, "be ready to leave him alone with this Word for a long time, willing to release him again in order that Christ may deal with him."[41] The Holy Spirit alone does that which we cannot and should not attempt to do.

The New Testament does not give us a single model or definitive, preconceived strategy for evangelization. The Christian's approach to the educated should remain completely flexible, open to the working and guidance of the Holy Spirit.

The Christian first asks, Am I really aware of the culture in which this educated is living? What is this person's inner thought-world? And how can my skills of lovingly listening improve so that I may establish a trust-relationship? Then, which of a variety of approaches might be most useful so that this particular individual will become accessible? What are the unique personal characteristics of this educated person, and what are the attendant implications for evangelization and education?

The spiritual journey begins. But you are not alone. You have Christ and his Word. The Holy Spirit is with you every step of the way. Do you really need anything more?

9
The Educated Today

We have been studying the educated, who they are, and how they can best be reached with the Gospel. Because our odyssey has spanned several decades, the question might be asked, "Are the educated today different from those of the last generation?"

The variety of responses that campus pastors gave will not be detailed here (cf. Appendix B). The worldviews and beliefs of the educated are as different as the persons holding them. Some today still hold to a purely scientific worldview. They are pragmatists, technologically-minded, and task-oriented. Their view, according to some analysts, seems to be dying because of a growing dependence on other epistemologies that acknowledge the less tangible aspects of life.

Others among the educated are protean, shifting constantly. They tend to debunk any attempts to define a coherent world-view, labeling such attempts as presumptuous.

Others seem to avoid fundamental issues of life, its meaning and purpose. One campus pastor reported, "Such students do not think!" Therefore they are not the truly *educated* as we have defined them.

Still others are confused. As compassionate Christians, we know they don't realize how self-centered they are. Persons of the New Age (almost unwittingly identifying themselves with God) are vigorously *channeling,* but don't realize they are in the wrong channel. Others in a sense of frenzied individual impotence end up in escapism, nihilism, or hedonism. Since there is no meaning anymore, they live for the day, the hour. A campus pastor wrote,

> Yet humanism still defines man for our world, and this definition still places the individual in the center of (one's) world. I believe the most accurate picture might be the "I" drawn and quartered in the rushing wheel of the modern world.

The point remains that theologically the human condition has not changed since the beginning of time. The great god is still *self*. It was *The Fall*, from Adam and Eve's succumbing to the tempter's words "you shall be as gods" (Gen. 3:5) down to Ayn Rand's ultimate "EGO!" (ending *Anthem*) to a blithely dancing, wide-eyed Shirley MacLaine on a TV special ebulliently announcing her not so new "discovery": "I AM GOD!"

Throughout our odyssey we have pinpointed the love of self as humanity's key problem. And whether it is seen in today's university student whose objective is career-success to make money, or the matron who admires Erica Jong, *self-absorption* is still the issue.

Being *curvatus in se* (curved in on on oneself) is still the basic dilemma of the *educated* today—and the apologist as well—as we struggle with the *peccator*, the sinful humanity, within us.

It is that self whom Christ came to redeem—by giving his own self for us on the cross. It is to him we must turn for rescue.

Are the educated today different from their forbears? Yes and no. They ask different questions. But their human condition remains the same. The ultimate questions have not changed. Their need for help from a Source outside themselves persists. For us the task remains: "Go ye therefore" with the message that "must be preached to all nations . . . repentance [*to*] the forgiveness of sins" (Luke 24:46-48. Cf. p. 128 above).

Epilog

The Christian apologist is keenly interested in the educated, since they are an integral part of our society. Their nature is complex, and yet they have not changed *essentially* since their counterparts lived during the Golden Age of Greece. They are still sinners in need of the grace of God.

The educated should be approached as *individuals*. Our contact point is their world, their questions. In his preaching and teaching ministry our Lord always began with the *known* in the hearer's world and moved to the unknown—the spiritual challenge he was bringing the person.

So our contact point with the educated becomes a conflict point as we present Christ, the scandal, the stumbling block, the one who hangs suspended at the very fulcrum of history.

Christ needs to be presented in terms of who he is for our chaotic generation. For he is discoverable and contemporary. *He* is the person each of us is to become, and the *power* to be that new creation—to become a "little Christ."

To leave behind one's cynical solipsism or self-satisfied humanism and surrender one's ego "to a little guy hanging on a cross 2000 years ago" is quite a step. But it is the challenge the Christian apologist brings. The educated may feint by acknowledging "the plague which affects us all." We point to each one's *personal* responsibility for sin, and that means facing the One sinned against.

The educated may fix on the repeated failures of the church as an institution. We say, focus on the "Failure" hanging on a cross. What will you do with him? Why does he still dominate all history?

The educated may ask, "How can a loving God let the innocent suffer?" We point to the Innocent One at Calvary and counter, "Why do you let him be crucified anew each day in your own life as you reject him? Weep not only for the oppressed. Weep for yourself, and change, turn around. Deal with your personal responsibility before God. Your own sin must be dealt with.

"So far in your life you have been drinking from a stream the source of which you deny. But one day that stream will flow no more for you. Today it is still available. When you drink of it, acknowledge its source, and by God's power turn your life in a different direction. Then you will find a living water in you which will last forever.

"It's not hidden. Go and find it. It's there in God's power supply of his Word and Sacraments and in the fellowship of educated persons like yourself who have had the intellectual integrity to admit their vulnerability and need to seek help outside themselves."

Our challenge to the educated must be presented with boldness, the *parresia* of the apostles. But it must also be with the *compassionate mind* of him whom we represent. Even in the face of rejection ours is the mind of Christ: "And he, beholding him, loved him."

For then they may see, like Danielle, the Heart of the Matter.

> God sacrificing Himself in that way, I guess that was the first thing that drew me to it. The enormity of that act. That, I think, is still the center of my faith. The fact that that cross is the center of the Faith.

Then they may sense the Presence, as C. S. Lewis's wife Joy Davidson discovered it. She thought, *if* God exists then there is nothing more important than my knowing about him. She began her search by reading C. S. Lewis and the Scriptures. *And God came in*. She was, she says, "The world's most surprised atheist."

Then they may be surprised by *joy*—like the man in *The Screwtape Letters* who burst out upon recognizing Christ, "So it was really *you* all the time!"

Absence of evidence is not evidence of absence. The *Deus absconditus* is the *Deus Revelatus*. The occasional silence of God is the silence *of* God. For he *does* speak to us in the living Word of his Holy Scriptures and in the personal witness in our day of intellectuals with faith who are "signposts along the way," challenging our hesitancy to commitment.

The educated cannot argue with our call to faith in Christ. They may deprecate it as a leap into the dark. But only when they have confronted him who went into the dark to die for our sins will they ever know any lasting peace.

Then they will discover that faith is not blind trust, but an enterprise placing us into the arms of a loving, forgiving God.

This God now calls us all to live for him, to risk and to dare. He challenges those who doubt: If any chooses to do God's will, that person will know the truth, whether it be of God (John 7:17).

With his compassionate mind God woos us to be truly educated. The exhilarating adventure begins with getting to know him personally in his Son Jesus Christ, the Mystery and the Hope of the world.

The Mystery and the Hope*

In reaching out
you are reached
In giving
you receive
In changing
you are changed
In loving
you are loved
In saving
you are saved
In serving
you are fulfilled
Christ in you
The mystery
and
the hope
of
the
world

Matt. 7:7–8; Col. 1:27

*Donald L. Deffner, *Please Talk to Me, God!* (St. Louis: Concordia, 1983), 109, with credit to Sharon Streater.

Appendix A

Student Projects in Reaching the Educated Adult: A Selected Sampling

Responses to Characters in Literature. Students imagine they are in conversation with the protagonists in a novel or play and relate their understanding of the Gospel to the characters' situation in life.

Ivan Denisovich by William Paterson
Jake in *The Sun Also Rises* by James T. Oldham
Siddhartha by Sharon Streater
Yossarian in *Catch 22* by Linda Regan

Reaching the Educated through the Liturgy by Roger Beese. A Lutheran seminarian discusses the appeal of liturgy to the aesthetic sensibilities of the educated.

A Response to Albert Camus by Tobina Dalton. A Methodist woman who served in the Resistance in the Netherlands in World War II challenges the anti-Christianity of Albert Camus.

The Gospel through Letters by Sue Barbian. A Lutheran woman examines the theological intricacies of writing letters to two close friends outside the church, seeking to contact "the natural depth of the soul"—that "faith might awaken faith."

A Letter to a Friend by John Mattson. A Lutheran shares his own doubts and struggles with an old friend but gently redirects him to the source of faith, the means of grace in the worshiping community.

Proclaiming God's Word to the Educated by Gilbert Holstein. A Lutheran professor highlights key homiletical points in reaching the educated and provides ten sermon outlines.

Reaching the Educated Adult in the Bible by Robert A. Atwood. A Lutheran teacher assesses the approaches used in the Scriptures to preach to, teach, and reach the educated adult. Featured analysis: the sermons in the book of Acts.

Putting Bible Study in Perspective by Jan Smith Wood. Seeing the Scriptures as icon rather than idol, an Episcopal woman proposes lay-led, small-group Bible study in parishioners' homes.

Science Fiction Literature and the Educated Person by Mark M. Stahnke. A Pacific School of Religion student analyzes science fiction as a medium of communication with the unchurched.

Let's Go to the Movies by Peter A. Zadeik, Jr. A Lutheran high school principal examines the fascination of movie-going in contrast to TV-viewing.

Church Advertising and the Educated Adult by John Miller. Which ads in local newspapers would appeal to the educated?

Robert Schuller and the Educated Adult by William Paterson. A very perceptive Baptist orthodontist and seminary student assesses the theology and methodology of a person on TV.

Reaching the "Needs" of the Educated by Betty Beckner. A suburban Congregational woman sees educated adults as sign posts rather than stumbling blocks and addresses their basic human needs as the contact point in reaching them.

After 30 Volkswagens: An Appropriate or Non-appropriate Exegesis of an Advertisement by John Cassidy. A Lutheran seminarian examines the subtle theological implications of magazine advertisements.

Reaching the Educated Adult in Our Community by W. R. Laws, Jr. A Presbyterian assesses how the people in his Indiana congregation might speak an authentic and relevant word to the educated in his community.

A Workshop for the Educated by Linda Regan. A Presbyterian woman treats "Your Gifts for Ministry." The Educated and the Identification of Gifts: A Workshop Design.

Contemporary Art as a Medium in Religious Communication with the Intellectual by Edward A. Brammer. A Lutheran illustrates the use of modern art in his parish as a bridge in reaching the intellectual.

Church Growth, Evangelism and Music by Doug Emigh. A Methodist layman describes how he and his choir became a "church within a church" through their rediscovery of the true ministry of music.

Personal Encounter: A Study in Christian Contemporary Music by Susan Davis. A recent convert describes her spiritual odyssey through the hippie movement, the peace and civil rights movements, and finally pantheism and the human potential movement to Christianity. Then through Christian rock music she demonstrates how others can be helped along a similar journey in their struggle after conversion, developing a relationship with Christ, and with *the big reach*—out to the Body of Christ in fellowship.

Lovers in a Dangerous Time: Attending to Rock 'n Roll in the Eighties by Brian S. Elster. A Lutheran seminarian attends to the "music of the age" that we might meet the One who "danced through every doorway" and "be filled with a music that bids us dance the dance of love."

The Political Person and the Church: Interviews, Analysis, Reflection by Sharon Streater. A Baptist woman shares her analysis of the unchurched political person's perception of the church, and sensitively demonstrates how "in reaching we are reached, in giving we receive, in changing we are changed, in saving we are saved, in transforming we are transformed."

Characteristics of the Educated Adult: Implications for the Church's Ministry by James T. Oldham. A Baptist pastor aptly summarizes thirteen common characteristics of the educated adult and suggests thirteen implications for the church's ministry of evangelization and education.

Appendix B

Responses of Campus Pastors

A questionnaire was sent to a number of campus-serving pastors throughout the United States asking about their ministry to the educated. What follows is a random sampling of their responses.

1. How do you see the thought-world of the educated today? How do they construct their lives and the world around them?

I seriously doubt whether one can speak of "the thought-world of the educated today." There are many thought-worlds among the educated and they are as different as the people holding them. There are some who still cling to a scientific worldview that holds tenaciously to the assumption that all truth must be arrived at scientifically with all that implies. But these seem to be a dying breed. It seems to be that there is a greater openness among the educated today to other epistemologies that would give greater acknowledgment to the less tangible (spiritual?) aspects of life. But this comes in varying degrees and in varying combinations. It is very difficult to categorize and stereotype the educated today.

They do not think! Generally they are taught to ingest and regurgitate information. The educational system, parents, and church have provided answers (that seldom work well as presented). This leads them on a binge to find the right "answer." Teens, students (grad and undergrad) and even faculty seldom think. Truly educated people have learned to think and apply God's Word to life. Application or common sense are the keys.

My sense of many university students—although that is not the exclusive focus of your survey—is that they have spent little time organizing any philosophy of life. They move from one class to the next, from one day to the next, often with little thought about issues any larger than what to do on Friday night or whether the corporate recruiter will offer an entry-level position. In campus ministry we work to expand those horizons, and find students willing to integrate faith and life, to consider the role of religion in a secular environment.

Whenever one is asked to speak in general terms about so varied a demographic group, gross generalizations are bound to appear. To minimize the "gross-ness" of my generalizations concerning the "educated," I suggest the following division: Pseudo-intellectuals, cynical intellectuals, and altruistic intellectuals. Pseudo-intellectuals get their news from *Time* magazine and ABC's *20/20.* They follow intellectual trends and so are assured of consuming the "right" ones. Cynical intellectuals read the entire *Wall Street Journal* and several other sources which can enlighten them concerning the human condition. They understand Pirandello and enjoy Hemingway. Scott Fitzgerald wrote about them in *This Side of Paradise*. They knew Watergate was no fluke and are gravely concerned about the military-industrial complex. Altruistic intellectuals have not yet been burned-out into their cynical counterparts. They are Christian or humanistic and hope to be able to help improve the world and the human condition. The Peace Corps is full of them.

Specialization embraces the definitions of the educated. Realizing that no one person can know everything, they concentrate on three areas of growth: educational/professional (the competency area they have chosen); interpersonal/family (relationships with others); and ego-centrical (personal identity/image/status/wealth). As a result people are not integrated into a community but are compartmentalized and have few "friends."

In our situation I see people who are technologically task-oriented. That might be due to one of the local institutions being an engineering school. Some of them are grappling with many of the questions of technology, particularly in the medical/biological field. How does a Christian come to grips with some of the technological advances we have made? All in all, the educated with whom I come in contact seem to be pragmatists. The worldview seems to be more "conservative" than it once was.

While there does not seem to be a monolithic philosophy among the educated on campus that is readily identified by people dropping the same name or reading the same books, there is a certain and identifiable "orthodoxy" and outward conformity to certain cherished dogmas, i.e., the feminist issues and the absolute insistence upon "inclusive" language; the cosmology which is a corollary of Darwinian evolution especially in terms of a relativistic approach to ethics; and a tendency to debunk any attempt at setting forth a coherent worldview (such attempts are deemed "presumptuous").

Consequently there is a narrow parochialism and departmentalism with little cross discipline engagement and certainly no attempts at grasping, let alone explaining the "big picture." As a corollary of this I see that the educated avoid dealing with fundamental concerns regarding the meaning and purpose of existence.

There is, of course, much to-do made about relevant and trendy political developments with a general and almost total dislike of the Reagan administration. Meaning, if there is any at all, seems to be a political concern and derived from the political sphere. Outside of a political world, career success, especially as measured by a particular income level attained, is a matter that occupies much of their attention.

I would observe that a good share of the profs think that life is finally meaningless and are simply going through the motions because it is the only thing available to bring home the paycheck. A spirit of cynical solipsism pervades much of university thought.

I believe there is a natural tendency to live in a frenzy, simply because the scientific and technological world has plunged us so rapidly (historically speaking) into a new economic era. The knowledge explosion is not that threatening to "uneducated" America, or even to typical blue-collar America (unless a job is lost), but the educated are aware of the rapid advances and feel a sense of individual impotence. Compensation (whether that is internally or externally motivated) becomes mandatory, and it takes the form of busywork, paperwork, committee meetings, and the like. Time for personal reflection and growth, family, and religion, and religion becomes the scapegoat. Yet humanism still defines man for our world, and this definition still places the individual in the center of his world. I believe the most accurate picture might be the "I" drawn and quartered in the rushing wheel of the modern world.

2. In your opinion, what major factors have brought about the worldview of the educated: political leaders, teachers, music, modern literature, TV, ads, newspapers, magazines, etc.?

College educated adults are often victims of atheistic instructors who have laughed at young adults in the final formative years of their faith-life. Instead of being stimulated to search for intellectual answers to their faith—and life— problems, they are drawn into the existentialist and atheistic worldview of humanism in its most secular garb. From that basis the literature, music, and the mass media (TV and national news organizations) underscore the basic feelings and directions received in the formative years.

I would suspect that the major contributors are within the academic community itself. Of course, teachers exert a great deal of influence with students. I would not want to discount the value of TV in shaping a worldview. It is quite subtle but powerful. Attitudes toward relationships with others often seem to reflect what is seen on TV and in movies. I rarely hear students discuss books they have read.

Television is possibly the most formative influence, in large degree because of the time exposed to it. Movies may be more of a factor than some of the printed materials, especially for the college students. The larger group of *educated* turns more to newspapers, magazines, journals, study groups. Many are involved in volunteer groups dealing with social issues, further sharpening their worldview (e.g., Habitat for Humanity, Lutheran Social Services).

An easy answer is the increased role of media in our lives, and that answer is not wholly incorrect. But I still believe media does more reflecting on our lives than creating reflections for us. Having worked in media, I know the frantic world it is, and there is precious little time for originating anything there. Under the media there is something much more important going on, made possible by communications technology. We live in a world of networks, in which an entire nation has an informational system that works horizontally. Exactly how it works is somewhat difficult to define. And under the networking, which is the means by which a modern view is transmitted, lies the ideological base and philosophical base. This is a complex base comprised of the elements of the kingdom of the left [political rulers, leaders] and the kingdom of the prince of darkness [Satan]. It is generated through various kinds of leadership—elected, self-appointed, and historically-fated. These minds consider current national mood (and now global mood) and legislate and administer according or not so accordingly.

Despair and ennui seem to contribute most to the present world-view of today's educated. Most cultural manifestations as per question 2 are reflections of the present worldview rather than formative of it. The loss of a sense of purpose and hope mostly shape the way people are viewing themselves and their world. Is not solipsism the last refuge of the hopeless?

As you might guess from the above, I do not believe that adults have a "single" worldview. Many, perhaps a majority, are influenced in their thinking and living by what they see others doing. Traditionally respected authority figures—be they political, religious, or educational—still carry weight with many people. But some are disenchanted with what they see and seek their own meaning. I suspect that the scientific revolution of the last 25 years or so has done more to unhinge life than anything else. Unfortunately the church and other major institutions of our society have done little to help people figure out how to live in a technological world which may blow itself up at any moment.

The mood of pessimism I see in many young people today is a reflection of that [worldview]. Many feel that they have little or no hope for a long future; hence the drive to "have it all now." Why bother to take care of the earth if the earth isn't going to be around in 25 years? People tend to view the problems of our world as being global (correctly) but therefore unsolvable (there's the rub). Where is hope in all this?

3. What are those elements which go into the decision-making of the educated? Is the head-trip of faith vs. reason over, is it all New Age and *me-generation, or what?*

Depending upon the answers derived from their college training, adults will either make a decision based upon their self-centeredness or upon their perceived understanding of altruism. Decision will ultimately be made for selfish reasons, since the individual is god. The dilemma of faith vs. reason is still very real.

Maybe *New Age* is big on the coasts, but not in the heartland. Me-generation is semi-over in terms of excessive individualism, but students continue to be very self-centered and materialist.

Some choose not to make decisions at all. They let others decide for them. Others are still into *me* thinking, perhaps allied with a few others who think (and act) like them. A few are seriously concerned with how their actions and decisions will affect others around the world. I see little evidence of *New Age* (whatever that is) in the people I work with. I do see people trying very hard to relate their faith to the struggles of everyday living and working.

In many ways our decision-making is governed by our technology. While I am not particularly given to Jacques Ellul's pessimism over the way *technique* dominates us, there is still much to it. The point would seem to be the "betterment of humanity" according to the highest sounding reasonings behind why we have decided to follow the paths we are on, but the bottom line continues more apparently to be the "comfort and self-gratifying sensuality" within which humanness is defined in terms of *self-fulfillment* and *happiness*.

Is there a sense of mission or purpose among the educated? Not that I've seen. Decisions seem to be made on the basis of career advancement or physical comfort. Many decisions made are ways to escape the unbearable boredom of having no theme to one's existence and hoping that a change in spouse, geography, occupation, etc. will give a focus to their lives. In terms of *New Age* the vocabulary and language on campus is notably different. People are using words such as *spiritual* and *mystical* which appears to me to be quite a departure from 10 years ago. Perhaps another attempt to carve out a sense of purpose?

4. What is the greatest mistake in evangelizing the educated? What do you feel is the best approach?

The greatest mistake is in assuming that all educated persons are alike and that there is one best approach for reaching them. The only "best approach" I can think of is to determine where that particular educated individual is and work from there. (You may want to take a look at David Dressel's article on "Faith, Intellect and

Evangelism" in the recently published *Faith and Intellect* study by The Lutheran Church—Missouri Synod's Office of Campus Ministry.)

Simple answers! Our simple evangelism outlines are geared to the blue-collar or no-collar worker. To approach the intellectuals of our day and age we must be speaking in the vocabulary of the times. (I wrote an article for the new journal *Evangelism* on Clement of Alexandria's evangelism method. He used the terms of his age and Christianized them.)

Faith is often presented as the opposite of intellectuality. Perhaps we must reiterate the truths of the earlier church fathers who stressed "faith-seeking understanding" in the Anselmian phrase, "I believe in order to understand."

The greatest mistake in evangelizing the educated is in trying to explain the foolishness of the Gospel. Erasmus of Rotterdam never fully understood it because he failed to fathom the magnitude of mankind's fall into sin. The best approach is to establish a relationship of mutual respect and then build on the authority of Scripture. The foolishness of God is wiser than man. If that point can be made, the Holy Spirit has a foundation from which to work. Genuine humility on the part of the person sharing Christ is the only hope for overcoming the pride of the educated unbeliever.

While the educated often look for proof, they are wise enough to realize that one cannot *prove* God or faith or other religious concepts. The best approach is to deal with faith as a faith issue, even if one discusses it rationally and logically. The flip side of this, especially today, is that some groups with the greatest success have all of the "proofs." This may say more about whether university students are *educated* than it says about anything else.

[The mistake would be in] approaching the unbeliever as if we are still sharing the same assumptions about the nature of reality. We are no longer fighting Voltaire and the enlightenment. We have lived through Feuerbach, Freud, Marx, Hegel, Nietzsche, and Sartre. The educated view the religious explanation of any aspect of reality, by definition, to be silly and a sure sign of mental deficiency. As a corollary of this I think the Christian propensity to make dogmatic assertions is most harmful until we have adequately shown that without a religious explanation of certain aspects of reality we are hard put to explain reality at all. (E.g., What explains the human intuition to be angry and fearful of death? The intuition is undeniable and yet based on an empirical assessment of life, death ought to be viewed as "the way the world turns." Yet all people everywhere view it as a damnable quirk in the whole business of living.)

Consequently I think that we must learn to ask sincere and pressing questions of the position of unbelief. Socratic dialog with the unbeliever—I have found insofar as I've employed the method—builds bridges to unbelief. Admittedly, it is much easier to speak in propositions rather than in the interrogative.

[The mistake is] assuming that we have all the answers or that we already know the questions. Both are presumptuous. My experience tells me that the only approach which has any hope of success is one of listening—finding out what their agenda is, struggling with them to relate faith and life, and being honest about the fact that I don't have all the answers either.

We are tempted, I think, to evangelize the educated by making the Christian faith reasonable, intellectually attractive, etc. I have problems with this method because it represents a "theology of glory."

I think the educated are reached, as are all humans, by story, by compassion, by the mischievous ways which the Gospel sneaks around our reason, intellects, etc., and explodes inside of our lives.

What I think might be unique about evangelism among the educated is this: the stories that break through might (not always) be related to their experience.

I am speaking from my very limited one-year experience as a campus pastor. I came thinking that I have to really sound learned and educated and rational. Already, I am discovering the educated to need a *playful gospel that sneaks* inside of them—in stories and pictures and life experiences.

[A mistake is] to try to reason and use logic. The best approach is the mystery of God's Word and Sacraments. A plain confession of the mystery of faith, from the cross to Trinity, makes the educated think on a different level.

[The mistake comes in] placating the desire for simplistic answers to questions about the meaning and purpose for human life. The approach must be grounded in the theology of the cross, not of glory. Educated people, too, are prone to synergistic schemes and reluctant to accept grace. Non-judgmental personal relationships are very important—much more so than literature.

Singling them out as somebody different [is a mistake]. Do not be afraid to call upon the educated. Do not fear their educated status. Most of the time they know very little about the Scriptures and the Christian faith.

The best approach—treat them like everyone else—but *be prepared—answer* their questions—pay some attention to them—tell them the truth of the claims of Scripture.

The greatest error is the evangelistic (not to be confused with *evangelical*) approach, as if the uneducated were automatically classed with either the unthinking or the less educated or both. The best approach is that of St. Paul on the Areopagus (Acts 17, 22–31). He used a courteous, reasoned approach; he quoted freely from contemporary (?) sources, and gently but clearly acknowledged his audience's intelligence. He called their thinking attention to a very obvious conundrum, and offered a solution for their consideration. The old rule in selling applies here as well: Meet them where *they* are.

5. What books would you use in evangelizing the educated?

If the educated's problems are of an intellectual nature, I still find the writings of C. S. Lewis helpful, particularly his *Mere Christianity*. Very often, however, we discover that the problems are not intellectual, but moral (having to do with lifestyle). The problem is not with the Creed but with the Ten Commandments.

My strategy has been to find out what folks are reading, read it myself, try to gather people together for conversation, and then try to relate the good news to what is being said. In our setting we've gathered people to read books on ecology, inter-faith dialogs, science fiction, various fields of biotechnology, ethics, and the meaning of higher education. Every conversation has been rich with opportunities to uncover and speak to the hurts of people.

I would recommend Paul L. Maier's *First Christmas, First Easter,* and *First Christians*. Also the writings of G. K. Chesterton, Paul Tournier, Helmut Thielicke, Dietrich Bonhoeffer's *Life Together* and *The Cost of Discipleship*, Kilpatrick's *The Emperor's New Clothes*, Muggeridge's *Jesus Rediscovered*, Koyama's *Water Buffalo Theology*, Martin E. Marty's short works on Scripture, Baptism and the Lord's Supper, Chad Walsh's *Campus Gods on Trial* and *Behold the Glory*, Dorothy Sayers' *A Matter of Eternity*, Josh McDowell's *Evidence That Demands a Verdict* and *Perspective* (Morse Press).

6. Do you find that many educated are readers? What do they read? Do you use modern secular literature and/or Christian writers in understanding and reaching the educated adult? What books and magazines would you recommend?

Decidedly *Yes!* That is probably what makes the educated different from those we consider their opposites. The educated continue their reading and studying all through life. Secular literature can have some benefits for the educated—especially if it is material which supports Christian views. *Harpers, Atlantic Monthly*, and other magazines of that calibre occasionally offer that.

The educated are readers, often voracious ones. A newspaper, a news magazine, a journal or two in areas of interest, usually a recent book on any of a number of topics. This again in contrast to students, many of whom read none of the above except as class assignments. I have often used the essays in *Time* on ethical issues for analysis papers in an ethics course, supplemented by leading questions to focus the response.

Books pertaining to a minute area of their discipline and on political concerns. Also books on investment, leisure activities, and humor. At our university the honors program heavily pushes the Great Books. I also read these books along with students and spent time helping them with their oral presentations and term papers. Most people assume the Great Books point forward to the present. We try to get our students to focus the discussion backward to the foundation of these books. We work on asking questions of the authors and of the class by using the characters of the classical novels and themes put forth in the other selections from the Great Books. We try to focus questions on how it was that people viewed their lives as purposeful while living under the sentence of non-existence.

Books and magazines—*Christian Century, Christianity Today, National Review, Religion and Society Report, The Family in America* are what I read regularly.

Post-graduates are readers; undergraduates are not (except, of course, for what is required). We have typically used a wide range of literature, secular and Christian, to try to stimulate interest in critical issues. As for books and magazines I would recommend - *Sojourners, The Other Side, Cultural Information Service,* and *Wittenberg Door*.

7. What do you find that is unique in preaching to the educated?

Law is always heard as law. There is really nothing that is unique in preaching to the educated, except that the Gospel may have to be even more clearly articulated than a simple John 3:16 statement. (But that is true for a parish pastor also.) Illustrations may come from more sophisticated sources and may be of a more mentally stimulating nature. Stories, however, work for all people.

Perhaps it is not unique, but their expectation of intellectual integrity and scriptural commitment.

Here at the Chapel my experience has been that the sermons which go over best are those in which I am in touch with issues and struggles of the people and am able to identify, sharpen those for them. They do not necessarily want answers, but they want to know that someone understands what they are thinking and feeling, and that someone is willing to walk with them in life.

The fact that you can *push* on the imagination, *press* beyond the obvious because they are used to *expanding* their minds. I think it is this possibility of moving from the purely personal to a more cosmic statement of faith, made possible by the "expansionable" mindset noted, that helps get some perspective on what it means to live in the world. That is not to forsake the individual or the personal, but to give it perspective and to help place it more properly.

8. What role do you see worship playing in reaching the educated adult?

I feel that the educated adult desires a variety of worship forms that are reasonably sophisticated and allow for a great amount of lay participation. Obviously, after a person has been evangelized there must be sufficient depth and breadth of worship life to satisfy his infant faith and assure him that there is room to grow and mature, as well.

Here is where our *evangelism* mindset has caused us to lose out with the intellectual/educated. We try to provide a "Protestant-type" of service which is of a touchy-feely nature and neglect the real awe and spiritual depth which our traditional (and catholic) liturgical heritage provides. Keep the liturgy! But do it well and with all reverence, pomp, and awe. (Many of the most educated people are turning from evangelical churches and joining the Roman or Anglican churches just because of their fuller liturgical forms.) We have so much!

The educated adult sees worship as an activity which also speaks to the emotional part of one's being: music, song, antiphonal reading, the sharing of bread and wine. While he or she is not searching for whatever *feels* good, there is nonetheless the recognition of something beyond the purely intellectual.

That depends, I am sure, on where the person is at a given moment. There is something about the awe and mystery of the faith that can be (not necessarily *is*) conveyed through the liturgy and I think that can be helpful in getting past the mere here and now. For that reason I am not particularly in favor of very specific, very concrete liturgies. They need the larger and more general world made available to them in the poetic function of liturgy so that it can be more *all-encompassing*. I do not, on the other hand, favor pageantry as an end in itself, lest that idea seem to be conveyed. I think liturgy can be done in a way that captures some of the sense of the awe and majesty of the presence of God without becoming overbearing or stiff or formal to the point of distancing one's self from the God whom we worship. When done properly, I think worship is a powerful witness for an educated adult, perhaps even more than the uneducated!

9. What materials do you use to get the educated into the Scriptures? What do you use for adult instruction of the educated?

Crossways! has proved to be an effective Bible study tool. Again, I use a good study Bible and a number of commentaries. For adult instruction we use a curriculum developed here and thoroughly padded by instructor comments. *The Book of Concord* is also used.

I highly recommend *Life with God* by Herman Theiss (Seven Hills Publishers, Suite 6, 131 30th N.E., Auburn, WA 98002). It has sold several hundred thousand copies by now. It has excellent true-false statements which really stimulate discussion!

10. What excites you most in your professional life right now?

It is *always* exciting to assure young people of God's forgiving love in Christ. Enabling students to care for others unconditionally is a challenge. We need to ask the Holy Spirit to help us demonstrate the fruit (Galatians 5) in all of our relationships.

What excites me most is that educated people are no different in their need for answers to the basic questions: Where did I come from? Why am I here? Where am I going? And the Gospel of Jesus Christ is the answer. I see it over and over. The Biblical message of sin and grace has power to convert, to comfort. There is no more exciting work!

[What excites me is] the openness of many people struggling for spiritual growth experiences. That openness is there for ministers who are not pretentious but enthusiastic about Jesus Christ—about the Gospel—and who convey a credible excitement and passion in the Christian faith. How to grow spiritually? Let the Spirit run and govern our lives. Practice both faith and love anywhere and anytime. Dare to invest our common faith in the lives of people of any race and culture who are needy and in trouble.

That which excites me most in my professional life right now is the opportunity that is mine to touch the lives of maturing young men and women so that Jesus Christ becomes a dynamic force in their believing, thinking, doing, and decision making. This excitement is heightened by the opportunity to be in contact with students from other countries, both Christian and non-Christian, supporting the Christian student in his/her faith in Christ, and opening the eyes of understanding of the non-Christians to the God who loves and cares for them. I rejoice over the student for whom Christ Jesus is a living Savior and Lord. I am depressed over the large numbers for whom Jesus has no special meaning in their lives.

Having come from a previous career, I absolutely love being a pastor because it is a professional life of studying and teaching. Everything that I do has this focus. To be able to serve the people whom God has chosen is also still a very exciting concept to me. I have been in the ministry five years and I have experienced no depressions. I am saddened at the many unbelievers in the world and at Christians who are able to make only a very shallow commitment to the Christian faith. We pastors must divorce ourselves somewhat from the modern worldview (especially from the rat race) and be examples of Christ-like living. That means we must be free of anxiety, greed for wealth, and self-centered living and be men of prayer, Bible study, and love. Love our wives and kids, parishioners, friends, enemies. I'm very excited about the ministry. There's so much work to be done. I'm confident that Christ will preserve his Church. The modern cultural environment in America is teaching us the absolute necessity of living by grace. That's scary, but it's what life in the church is all about.

Appendix C

Trends

(The following was provided in a mailing by Rev. Ed Schmidt, Campus Ministry Counselor, The Lutheran Church—Missouri Synod, May, 1987.)

Are there some trends in campus ministry? We might take note of a few, gleaned from conversations with you—and with others in campus ministry, and noted also in various campus ministry reports; and gleaned also from the comments you shared on your conference registration forms.

1. Commuter students are increasing dramatically. Living at home for many students has become a financial necessity.

2. More and more students have part-time jobs because of increasing financial burdens.

3. Tuition costs are going out of sight (*Newsweek* article). Total annual package for Ivy League schools now averages more than $17,000.

4. The ethnic mix on campus is becoming more and more diverse. (Speak with Dennis Tegtmeier/University of California-Irvine, a school that is 40% Oriental.)

5. The day of the student who graduated from high school and goes straight through four years of parent-supported schooling is going the way of the dinosaur.

6. More than half of the students of the 1990s will come from single-parent families.

7. Para-church groups nationally are losing membership. Gordon MacDonald, national president of Inter-Varsity Christian Fellowship, reports that IV has declined in membership dramatically during the last five years.

8. Alcohol abuse continues to climb. Partying on many campuses

begins already on Thursday night—an added incentive for trying hard not to schedule classes on Friday. Alcoholism is on the increase as well.

9. Students today, from what you tell me, continue to be extremely career-oriented—extremely materialistic—lacking the world-changing idealism of the 60's. The supreme goal is a good-paying job and the security to enjoy the good things of life—as long as the world lasts!

10. Students today appear to be less *small-group* oriented—and more *event* oriented—which may have something to say about the reluctance of students to do anything on a regular basis—like worship. What seems to appeal is *group-oriented entertainment*.

11. The unchurched segment of the student population is growing each year. Estimates continue to indicate that the average student body is at least 70% unchurched.

12. The average age or the *mean* of the student body continues to climb—many student bodies showing a mean of 25 to 28 years of age.

13. Peer ministry—student-to-student ministry—is growing and appears to be more effective than minister-to-student ministry.

14. You keep telling me that when observing students, what you see on the outside is not what's on the inside, that thousands of confident-appearing students are desperately hurting within (Depression/16 suicides at University of Minnesota).

15. Enthusiasm for campus ministry continues to diminish in the church. Campus ministry no longer occupies a strategic role in the eyes of the parents and students and local parishes. It apparently must be sufficient for a student to maintain a strong spiritual life if he/she returns home once a month to worship with the family in the "home church."

16. Fewer students seem genuinely interested in church attendance or in Christian worship, much less in participation in campus ministry programs. Increasingly we are working only with the truly committed ones!

17. Denominational loyalties continue to fade as students reveal less and less interest (in general) for studies of church-body creedal statements, but, strangely enough, reveal a growing interest in in-depth doctrinal studies. (Some of you are even teaching beginning Greek to your students!)

18. Our congregations continue to experience heavy losses in the post-confirmation and high school age group, the group we are expected to reclaim and renew during their college years.

19. Ignorance of the university as a mission field and the incredible opportunities for mission, displayed by members of our congregations, continue to plague us.

20. There is an increasing aggressiveness among religious groups other than Christian, particularly the Muslims. The Muslim goal: a Muslim worshiping community, together with a worship center or mosque on every major campus in this country by the year 2000.

21. An increasing awareness in the university community that Roman Catholics and Lutherans consistently and persistently maintain strong campus ministries, while most main-line demoninations are inconsistent at best.

22. The apparent trend is not toward more permissive sex, even though couples continue to live together *unmarried*—a real problem for us in premarital counseling. The trend is toward *responsible* sex, according to Dr. Ruth, whatever that is. Fifty-six percent of university students think that sex before marriage is always wrong. Ninety-five percent believe that extra-marital sex is always wrong.

23. The institutional church seems to be increasingly out of touch with the realities facing students today and the student graduates. It's tough to be a student and to interpret that for parents or for the church!

24. Too many students continue to describe their worship experience (in their home church, obviously) as *boring*, uninteresting, without *aliveness*. A tremendous challenge for us in campus ministry.

***Trends* Update, March 1989**

25. Denominational student organizations appear to be "in" again. Methodists, Episcopalians, Baptists, and others have experienced a resurgence of denominational loyalty and enthusiasm among students in sufficient measure to warrant the establishment of *student groups.*

26. The presence on our nation's campuses of more than 350,000 foreign or international students continues to provide dramatic op-

portunities for *international friendship* and the proclaiming of the Good News under the direction of the Holy Spirit.

27. Creative programs by colleges and universities, both public and private, four-year and two-year, are attracting hundreds of new students of all ages. Enrollments, predicted by many to decline, have instead topped 12 million throughout the 1980s and in this current year alone (1988–89) rose 2.4 percent to a record 12.8 million students. The opportunities for Christian outreach on our nation's campuses are incredible.

28. Racial tension, accompanied by a marked intolerance, appears to be increasing on campuses, not only between groups of different color and creed, but between groups with differing moral values, political persuasions, and degrees of affluence.

29. It is becoming increasingly difficult for campus ministers to *build community* among students. Most students are pulled in so many different directions by studies, employment, life-style, daily class schedules, and social routines and, as a result, are so *fragmented* that bringing them together in *community* with any degree of regularity seems almost out of the question.

30. The sometimes dramatic (even *outlandish*) changes among youth in current *fashions* and *hair styles,* with the accompanying short-term *fads* of the day, are no longer signaled by the college crowd, but demonstrated among high school youth instead.

Notes

Introduction

1. Virgilia Petersen, quoted in "Messengers of Peace," unpublished essay by Robert K. Menzel at the PTR Mission to Ministers, Los Angeles, CA, 1959.
2. Joel H. Nederhood, *The Church's Mission to the Educated American* (Grand Rapids: Wm. B. Eerdmans, 1960), 124.
3. Anthony T. Padovano, *The Estranged God: Modern Man's Search for Belief* (New York: Sheed and Ward, 1966), 166.
4. J. B. Phillips, *God Our Contemporary* (New York: Macmillan, 1960), 131.
5. R. W. B. Lewis, *The Picaresque Saint: Representative Figures in Contemporary Fiction* (New York: J. B. Lippincott, 1961), 59.

Chapter 1: Who Are the "Educated"?

1. Joel H. Nederhood, *The Church's Mission to the Educated American* (Grand Rapids: Wm. B. Eerdmans, 1960), 53–60, 123–124.

Chapter 2: Books to Make Us Think

1. Joel H. Nederhood, *The Church's Mission to the Educated American* (Grand Rapids: Wm. B. Eerdmans, 1960).
2. Nederhood, 141.
3. Nederhood, 153.
4. Cf. the author's review in *Concordia Theological Monthly,* XXXII, 4 (April 1961), 251–252.
5. Nederhood, 103.
6. Nederhood, 11.
7. Nederhood, 66.
8. Nederhood, 148–149.
9. Nederhood, 157. In later years Joel H. Nederhood became the Broadcast Minister of the Christian Reformed Church.
10. Anthony T. Padovano, *The Estranged God: Modern Man's Search for Belief* (New York: Sheed and Ward, 1966).
11. Padovano, 56.
12. Padovano, 159. Cf. especially the summaries, 157–158.
13. Padovano, 177.
14. Padovano, 281.

15. Padovano, 283–284.
16. Padovano, 285.
17. Padovano, 54.
18. Padovano, 166.
19. Padovano, 47.
20. Padovano, 63.
21. Padovano, 278.
22. Padovano, 76–77.
23. Albert Camus, *The Plague* (New York: Modern Library, 1948), 195–197. Copyright by Stuart Gilbert.
24. Camus, 228–229.
25. Camus, 116–113.
26. Padovano, 177.
27. Anthony Gibson, *The Silence of God* (New York: Harper & Row, 1969). Gibson sees a note of evolutionary hope in the films he selected, but Bergman himself said in an interview at age 65: "It is impossible and absurd to have [a philosophy of life]. [He roars with laughter.] . . . I'm not dogmatic at all, I've got one basic view: to have no basic views" (*Datebook*, the *San Francisco Chronicle*, July 8, 1984, p. 21).
28. Gibson, 12.
29. Elie Wiesel, *Night* (New York: Bantam Books, 1982), 62.
30. The title of a book by Francis Schaeffer (Downers Grove: InterVarsity, 1968). Cf. also his *Escape from Reason*.
31. John Powell, *A Reason to Live! A Reason to Die!* (Niles: Argus Communications, 1975). At this writing the book has remained in print since 1972. Powell is also the author of *Why Am I Afraid to Tell You Who I Am? Why Am I Afraid to Love?* and *Unconditional Love*, and a number of talks available on cassette.
32. Powell, 9.
33. R. W. B. Lewis, *The Picaresque Saint* (New York: J. B. Lippincott, 1956), 79. The quote continues: "[This God] had been created in the polemics of Martin Luther. Cf. Lewis' explication of this comment in footnote 24, pp. 301–302. Christians must also cope with Nietzsche's comment: "If Christians wish us to believe in their Redeemer, why don't they look more redeemed?" (Lewis, 62).
34. Powell, 33.
35. C. S. Lewis, *Mere Christianity* (New York: Macmillan, 1977).
36. C. S. Lewis, *The Screwtape Letters* (New York: Macmillan, 1964).
37. Available from Lord and King Associates, 28W120 Robin Lane, West Chicago, IL 60185.
38. 1986, San Francisco Theological Seminary, San Anselmo, CA. A major resource for research on C. S. Lewis (and the books and papers of Owen Barfield, G. K. Chesterton, George MacDonald, Dorothy L. Sayers, J. R. R. Tolkien, and Charles Williams) is The Marion E. Wade Center, Dr. Lyle W. Dorsett, Director, Wheaton College, Wheaton, IL 60187-5593. Telephone: 312-260-5908. Also see Kathyrn Lindskoog, *C. S. Lewis: Mere Christian* (Wheaton: Harold Shaw Publishers, 1987). To Lindskoog C. S. Lewis wrote: "You know my work better than anyone else I have met."

39. J. B. Phillips, *Plain Christianity* (New York: Macmillan, 1954).
40. J. B. Phillips, *God Our Contemporary* (New York: Macmillan, 1960).
41. Phillips, 6.
42. Phillips, especially 6-11.
43. Phillips, 130.
44. Phillips, 118, 130–131.
45. John 7:17.
46. Chad Walsh, *Campus Gods on Trial* (New York: Macmillan, 1962).
47. Chad Walsh, "Remarks on 'The Church and the Intellectual,'" unpublished paper from the Commission on College and University Work, The Lutheran Church—Missouri Synod, St. Louis, Mo.
48. Ibid.
49. Walsh, *Campus Gods on Trial,* 117ff.
50. Walsh, 87.
51. William E. Diehl, *Christianity and Real Life* (Philadelphia: Fortress Press, 1976). Cf. also his *Thank God It's Monday* (Fortress Press, 1982); *In Search of Faithfulness: Lessons from the Christian Community* (Fortress Press, 1987) has as its theme practicing Christian faithfulness in the business world in the face of the church's own barriers to developing faith. Diehl was manager of sales for the Bethlehem Steel Corporation and a member of the executive council of the Lutheran Church in America.
52. J. Russell Hale, *The Unchurched: Who They Are and Why They Stay Away* (San Francisco: Harper & Row, 1977). My quotations are from the first version, *Who Are the Unchurched?* (Atlanta: Glenmary Research Center, 1977).
53. For more detail see my chapter "Education for Evangelization," in Marvin L. Roloff, ed., *Education for Christian Living* (Minneapolis: Augsburg Publishing House, 1987), 102.
54. In this connection cf. Arlon K. Stubbe, *The Phantom Church: How to Minister to Potential Dropouts* (Lima: C. S. S. Publishing Company, 1986) on recognizing potential dropouts; also John S. Savage, *The Apathetic and Bored Church Member* (LEAD Consultants, Inc., P. O. Box 311, Pittsford, N.Y. 14534, 1976). For the statistic-minded person this is a challenging text on the psychological and theological dynamics that occur in the life of a church member who is active, then two or three years later inactive.
55. Hale, 44.
56. Hale, 84–85.
57. Hale, 44.
58. Ibid.
59. Grand Rapids: William B. Eerdmans, 1986.
60. Philadelphia: Fortress Press, 1972.
61. New York: Greenwood, 1981. Two other comments of Hale are noteworthy: "The particular *culture* determines the *language* and the *ethos* by which the church communicates the faith." "Evangelization is the *raison d'etre* of the whole people of God."
62. Edward A. Rauff, *Why People Join the Church* (New York: Pilgrim Press, 1980 and Atlanta: Glenmary Research Ct., 1979). My references are from the latter

text. Rauff did an excellent study in the course Reaching the Educated Adult on "One Minute Spot Announcements for Radio" in the summer of 1966.

63. Rauff, 155.
64. Rauff, 118. Emphasis mine.
65. Rauff, 120.
66. Ibid. Note once again, we must dismantle the educated's misconceptions about Christianity.
67. Rauff, 120–121.
68. Rauff, 121.
69. Rauff, 120–121.
70. Sheldon Vanauken, *A Severe Mercy* (New York: Harper & Row, 1977), 85.
71. Rauff, 123.
72. Rauff, 128.
73. Ibid.
74. Richard Lischer, *Speaking of Jesus: Finding the Words for Witness* (Philadelphia: Fortress Press, 1982).
75. Cf. also Richard Lischer, *A Theology of Preaching* (Nashville: Abingdon, 1981).
76. Lischer, *Speaking of Jesus,* x.
77. Lischer, 7–8.
78. Lischer, 56.
79. Lischer, 66.
80. Lischer, 68.
81. Wheaton: Tyndale House, 1982.
82. Minneapolis: Augsburg, 1981.
83. New York: Paulist Press; Grand Rapids: Eerdmans, 1975.
84. St. Louis: Concordia Publishing House, 1986.
85. St. Louis: Concordia Publishing House, 1987.
86. Fullerton, CA: R. C. Law & Co., 1987.
87. Downers Grove: InterVarsity, 1979.
88. Philadelphia: Fortress Press, 1981.
89. St. Louis: Concordia Publishing House, 1988.

Chapter 3: Modern Literature and the Educated

1. To develop skill in evaluating literature and using it as an evangelistic tool, students in class were asked to pick a character in a novel and set up a dialog with the individual or write an imaginary letter to him/her.
2. A. L. Kershaw, et al., *Alone in the Crowd* (New York: National Student Council of the YMCA and YWCA, 1954), 7.
3. William R. Mueller, *The Prophetic Voice in Modern Fiction* (New York: Association Press, 1959). While lecturing for the chief of chaplains office at Eielson AFB in Alaska I promoted his book; one Air Force wife went out and read six

novels as a result. She wrote Mueller, and he wrote me in appreciation.

4. Mueller, 23.
5. Mueller, 24.
6. Mueller, 14.
7. Mueller, 16.
8. See classic examples of this in William H. Whyte, Jr., *The Organization Man* (Garden City: Doubleday Anchor Books, 1956); also, Sloan Wilson, *The Man in the Grey Flannel Suit* (New York: Simon & Schuster, 1955).
9. Halford Luccock, *Communicating the Gospel* (New York: Harper & Brothers, 1954), 97. (This "Simeon Stylites" of *The Christian Century* as early as 1934 wrote a book titled *Contemporary American Literature and Religion*.)
10. "The New Age and the New Man" in *The Pulpit* (Willet, Clark & Company), XXIX (July 1958), 20.
11. Albert Camus, *The Fall* (New York: Alfred A. Knopf, 1958), 58.
12. Robert E. Fitch, "Secular Images of Man in Contemporary Literature," *Religious Education*, LIII (March–April, 1958), 89. I am indebted to my Graduate Theological Union, Berkeley, colleague for this watershed article, an early catalyst for the flood of "theology and modern literature" books.
13. William Mueller, op. cit., 109, writing about Franz Kafka, *The Trial* (New York: Alfred A. Knopf, 1937).
14. Jean-Paul Sartre, *No Exit and Three Other Plays* (New York: Vintage Books, 1960), 47.
15. Ibid.
16. William Inge, *The Dark at the Top of the Stairs* (New York: Random House, 1958).
17. James Cozzens, *By Love Possessed* (New York: Harcourt, Brace, and Company, 1957), 256.
18. Robert E. Fitch, op. cit., 85.
19. Arthur Miller, *Death of a Salesman* (New York: Viking Press, 1958), 133.
20. Ibid., 138.
21. Robert E. Fitch, op. cit., 87.
22. Richard H. Luecke, "The 'Atheology' of Tennessee Williams," *Present Day Issues in the Light of Faith* (Chicago: Commission on College and University Work, 1960-196l), 1. Source not given.
23. Robert E. Fitch, op. cit., 87–88.
24. J. D. Salinger, *The Catcher in the Rye* (New York: Signet Books, 1960), 91.
25. Salinger, 156.
26. Joel H. Nederhood, op. cit., 114.
27. Quoted in *Six Great Modern Short Novels* (New York: Dell Publishing Company, 1954), 56.
28. Ibid.
29. Quoted in the *St. Louis Post-Dispatch*, Jan. 17, 1960.
30. Albert Camus, op. cit., 58.
31. Joel H. Nederhood also points out the refusal of many contemporary persons to admit responsibility for *individual* guilt, 132.

32. Albert Camus, op. cit., 147, 132.
33. Steve Tollefson, a writing instructor at UC Berkeley, recently surveyed 682 freshmen on what they had last read for pleasure. He found that the most popular book was Alice Walker's *The Color Purple*. The author mentioned most often was Steven King, followed by Danielle Steel, Sidney Sheldon, Robert Ludlum, and Jean Auel. Most popular authors of "classics" were Kurt Vonnegut, George Orwell, and John Steinbeck.
34. A. E. Housman, *Collected Poems* (New York: Buccaneer Bks., 1983).
35. Cf. Finley Eversole, "Art in the Pulpit," *The Pulpit*, XXXI (Dec. 1960), 7–10.
36. Sidney Lanier, "The Gospel According to Freud," *Christianity and Crisis*, XCIII (April 14, 1958), 51.
37. Ibid., 51–52.
38. I believe *The Devil's Advocate* is still his best book.
39. William Mueller, op. cit., 14.
40. 2 Cor. 5:17. Living out the "Christ-person" is no mere *imitatio Christi*, but being plunged through Baptism into death with him and rising with the resurrected Christ, who now lives within the Christ-person. Cf. Col. 3:11b (Goodspeed): "Christ is everything and in us all" and Rom. 6:3–9.
41. Phillips, *Letters to Young Churches* (1947), Eph. 4:17–27.
42. Andrew Greeley, *The Cardinal Sins* (New York: Warner Books, 1984), 399–400.
43. Op. cit., 350.
44. This is not to deny the need to examine and affirm the sexual nature of humanity—a subject often feared or ignored or avoided. I merely point up Greeley's seeming obsession with the sex lives of priests and the prurient responses of his readers.
45. Andrew Greeley, "Fiction in the Religious Imagination," (*America*, April 6, 1985).
46. New York: Pocketbooks, 1987.
47. R. W. B. Lewis, *The Picaresque Saint* (New York: J. B. Lippincott, 1961), 258.
48. William Mueller, op. cit., 16. Also see John D. Crossan, *The Dark Interval: Towards a Theology of Story* (Sonoma: Polebridge Press, 1988); Robert Detweiler, *Religious Readings in Contemporary Fiction* (San Francisco: Harper & Row, 1989); Carl Ficken, *God's Story and Modern Literature: Reading Fiction in Community* (Philadelphia: Fortress Press, 1985); Northrop Frye, *The Great Code: The Bible in Literature* (New York: Harcourt, Brace, 1983); and David Tracey, *The Analogical Imagination* (New York: Crossroad, 1985). For a listing of Christian novelists, poets, and writers, write to Karen L. Mulder, Christians in the Arts Networking, P.O. Box 1941, Cambridge, MA 02238-1941.
49. In this connection see also J. B. Phillips' *God Our Contemporary*, 130.
50. R. W. B. Lewis, *The Picaresque Saint* (New York: J. B. Lippincott, 1961), 58, 97.
51. Lewis, op. cit., 58. For these brief insights into Camus's work I am indebted to this classic study of R. W. B. Lewis, who knew Camus personally. Lewis used the generic term "man."
52. Lewis, op. cit., 299.
53. Lewis, op. cit., 61.

54. *The Myth of Sisyphus*, quoted in Lewis, op. cit., 62.
55. Lewis, op. cit., 52–63, with the latter quote from *Noces*.
56. Lewis, op. cit., 64.
57. Lewis, op. cit., 65, 67, 68.
58. Lewis, op. cit., 71, 73.
59. Lewis, op. cit., 73, 76, 77.
60. Lewis, op. cit., 78–79.
61. Lewis, op. cit., 83. Thus also ended *The Fall*, with the "icy cold absence of God" (Lewis).
62. Quoted in Lewis, op. cit., 88.
63. Lewis, op. cit., 89.
64. Lewis, op. cit., 91.
65. Lewis, op. cit., 101.
66. Lewis, op. cit., 108.
67. Quoted in the *St. Louis Post Dispatch*, Jan. 17, 1960.
68. Luke 15:17.
69. Tobina Dalton, unpublished manuscript in the course Reaching the Educated Adult, Pacific Lutheran Theological Seminary, Berkeley, CA., Spring 1979.
70. Ibid.
71. Ibid.
72. Dr. Rieux, the unbelieving physician in *The Plague*.
73. P. Kuhn, *Gottes Selbsterniedrigung in der Theologie der Rabbinen* (1968).
74. Elie Wiesel, *Night*. (New York: Bantam Books, 1982), 62.
75. Tobina Dalton, ibid. The moral problem created by the German habit of executing innocent hostages is not mentioned. The Resistance fighter always risked having on his conscience the death of so many people, executed as a direct result of his act of sabotage.
76. Lewis, op. cit., 99.
77. Lewis, op. cit., 79.
78. Cf. John T. Pless, "Martin Luther: Preacher of the Cross," *Concordia Theological Quarterly*, 51 (April–June 1987), 2–3.

Chapter 4: Characteristics of the Educated Adult

1. Marvin W. Anderson, ed. *The Gospel and Authority: A P. T. Forsyth Reader* (Minneapolis: Augsburg, 1971), 197.
2. Used by permission. At this writing James T. Oldham is Chief, Recruitment and Ecclesiastical Relations Division, Office of the Command Chaplain, Air Reserve Personnel Center, Denver, CO. In this position he manages the chaplain candidate program for the USAF and recruits to fill vacancies in the reserve chaplaincy.

   In my current teaching I have compiled a sourcebook of readings comprising some two dozen student papers. They stand out among the several hundred I have kept over the twenty-eight years of teaching Reaching the Educated Adult. They are listed in Appendix A.

3. Jerold W. Apps, *How to Improve Adult Education in Your Church* (Minneapolis: Augsburg, 1972), 10ff.
4. Robert S. Clemmons, *Education for Churchmanship* (Nashville: Abingdon, 1966), 63.
5. Paul Bergevin and John McKinley, *Adult Education for the Church* (St. Louis: Bethany Press, 1970), 3–4.
6. See Appendix B, Campus Pastors' Responses, questions 5 and 6.

Chapter 5: Preaching to the Educated

1. Nederhood, op. cit., 141.
2. See Appendix B, Campus Pastors' Response, questions 7 and 8.
3. Nederhood, op. cit., 144–147.
4. Job, chapters 38-40, a crucial text in preaching the doctrine of creation to the educated.
5. Colossians 1:16 (Phillips).
6. Wayne Saffen, "The Mission of the Church to Higher Education," 2. Unpublished manuscript.
7. For illustrations citing modern literature in preaching to the educated see Richard Andersen and Donald L. Deffner, *For Example: Illustrations for Contemporary Preaching* (St. Louis: Concordia Publishing House, 1977).
8. Psalm 51:4.
9. "The Faith of Great Scientists," *The American Weekly* (New York: Hearst Publishing Co. 1948), 33–34. Cf. also Roy Abraham Varghese, ed., *The Intellectuals Speak Out about God: A Handbook for the Christian Student in a Secular Society* (Dallas: Lewis and Stanley, 1984).
10. Luke 15:37 (Phillips).
11. Warren Schmidt, in Donald L. Deffner, ed., *Toward Adult Christian Education*, op. cit., 31.
12. From Elizabeth Elliott, "The Ones Who Are Left," *Christianity Today,* Feb. 27, 1976, 7, also quoted in a sermon on loneliness by the writer, "Not Invited to the Party?" *The Concordia Pulpit* (St. Louis: Concordia Publishing House, 1982), 74–79.
13. Heb. 13:5.
14. See Walsh, op. cit., 146–148.
15. See Hale, op. cit.
16. Gilbert Holstein, "Proclaiming God's Word to the Educated." Unpublished manuscript for the course The Campus Ministry.
17. Note Walsh's beautiful statement how God gives back our "I," our self, and "what began as surrender to a master ends as sonship to a father." Op. cit., 87.
18. See the excellent analysis of this distinction by Donald R. Heiges in *The Christian's Calling* (Philadelphia: Fortress Press, 1984).
19. Sharon Streater, "The Political Person and the Church: Reaching and Being Reached." Unpublished manuscript for the course Reaching the Educated Adult, 8.

20. Ibid.
21. Sharon Streater, op. cit., 11.
22. Sharon Streater, op. cit., 13.
23. See Nederhood, op. cit., 122–123, 140–141.
24. From a conversation with Harry Mumm, Pacific Lutheran Theological Seminary, Berkeley, CA.
25. See David P. Scaer, "Sanctification in Lutheran Theology," *Concordia Theological Quarterly*, 49 (April–July 1985), 181. Scaer notes Martin Luther's stress on the positive prescription rather than the negative prohibition of the Decalog (184).
26. Einar Billing, *Our Calling* (Philadelphia: Fortress Press, 1964).
27. The foregoing section on "The Message to Be Preached" is taken from Donald L. Deffner, *A Primer/Primer for Preaching* (Fort Wayne: Concordia Theological Seminary Press, 1988), 15–16. The text deals with the theological, the dialogical, and the methodological in homiletics. Cf. especially the chapter contributed by Philip Molnar on "Today's Pulpit and Contemporary Society."

Chapter 6: The Educated and the Bible

1. *Ministries with Young Adults,* produced by the Division of Parish Services, Lutheran Church in America (Philadelphia, 1987). The style of worship, pastors' sermons, location of the church, and involvement of other young adults were also cited as reasons for affiliating.
2. Roland Seboldt, in Donald L. Deffner, ed., *Toward Adult Christian Education*, op. cit., 69.
3. Jan Smith Wood, "Putting Bible Study in Perspective." Unpublished manuscript for the course Reaching the Educated Adult.
4. Robert A. Atwood. Unpublished manuscript, 8–9.
5. Ibid.
6. Diehl's phrase, "The laity must be the agents of their own formation."
7. A phrase of Randolph Crump Miller's.
8. "An adult education program presupposes that new days call for new responses both for the church and for individuals, and that change can take place. . . . Education allows adults to be better decision-makers as they attempt to interpret the will of God in the light of the experiences of life." John Lundin, "Focus on Adult Education," in Richard Olson, ed., *The Pastor's Role in Educational Ministry* (Philadelphia: Fortress, 1974), 47–55. I use this excellent chapter in each course I teach in education.
9. Walter J. Schedler, "A Bridge for Mission Work Today: Lessons from St. Paul." Unpublished manuscript, Concordia Theological Seminary, Fort Wayne, IN, Jan. 27, 1986.
10. Walter J. Schedler, op. cit., 2, says, ". . . along with their church's basic Biblical philosophy, *sola Scriptura, sola gratia, sola fide, soli Deo gloria.*"
11. Ibid., 10.
12. "The resource is the living rooms and kitchens of the homes of the congregation. The most beautiful and natural place for the Gospel is ordinary folk in

honest communication in their homes talking and listening to one another about what really matters in life. . . . To become equal, to divest myself of any 'expert' status. I come not to get or want anything but to understand and to care." Gerhard Knutson, *Listening Witness,* an outline of procedures for evangelism at St. James Lutheran Church, Crystal, Minnesota. Mimeographed paper distributed through ALC Evangelical Outreach training events, 1978, page 3.

"Evangelism is the communication of the whole Gospel. Grace to man is spoken to the whole man. It is a manifestation of the grace which is in Christ Jesus to show love both to the body and to the soul, for the body and the soul are simply different ways to speak of the same whole person. . . . Whatever you do in the name of Jesus is a proclamation of the grace manifested in Christ Jesus. . . . If you treat every human being in a human way, if you can make a person whole in his spirit, give him hope, train him to become proud of his identity, help him to care for himself and his work, whatever you do to make the Gospel alive, you proclaim the grace of God manifested in Christ Jesus." Dr. Kent S. Knutson, "What Evangelism Is," an address to the 1972 ALC convention, as quoted in *Gospel, Church, Mission* (Minneapolis: Augsburg, 1976), 138.

Chapter 7: The Case Study

1. This case was prepared by Donald L. Deffner of Pacific Lutheran Theological Seminary, Berkeley, CA, as a basis for class discussion rather than to illustrate either effective or ineffective handling of an administrative situation. Copyright 1974 by The Case-Study Institute. Distributed by the Intercollegiate Case Clearing House, Soldiers Field, Boston, MA 02163. All rights reserved to the contributors. Printed in the U.S.A.

Chapter 8: Building Trust with the Educated

1. Donald L. Deffner, *Bold Ones on Campus* (St. Louis: Concordia, 1973).
2. Florist John Ortner, an enthusiastic lay Lutheran evangelist in the Pacific Northwest, defines evangelization as the *personal* and *explicit* communication of the Gospel. He feels the newest converts to Christianity are the best evangelists. In his opinion, only ten percent of the people in a parish have the personality/gifts to make doorbell-type calls. Only five percent are doing it. We need to identify the other five percent and train them. And, he says, "Let's not bug the other ninety percent to do that which they don't have the gift to do. They can do other things in the church." He lists types of survey calls as (1) visitor, (2) inactives, (3) unchurched. Twenty to thirty out of 100 calls are worth a 7–10 day later follow-up call. After people miss church four times they get a call: "We've missed you." Four reasons for inactives are (1) the pastor—the most visible to stub your toe on; (2) another member; (3) family split; (4) burnout—they've been on every committee; they're overused.
3. The title of a devotional classic by Herman W. Gockel that has sold several hundred thousand copies (St. Louis: Concordia, 1956).
4. Note Abraham Maslow's levels of need: physiological, security, social, ego, self-actualization, aesthetic, intellectual. Cf. also Warren Schmidt, "The Churchman and the Social Sciences," in *Toward Adult Christian Education: A Symposium*,

Donald L. Deffner, ed. (River Forest, IL), 19th Yearbook of the Lutheran Education Association, 1962), 30.

5. Cf. Margaret Wold, *The Critical Moment* (Minneapolis: Augsburg, 1978).
6. Promotional comments on jacket of Harry A. DeWire, *The Christian as Communicator* (Philadelphia: The Westminster Press, 1961).
7. DeWire, op. cit., 17–19; 26–27.
8. DeWire, op. cit., 22–25; 27.
9. You could always expect some jokers to sign their cards *church preference—Gothic; race—human.*
10. Warren H. Schmidt, op. cit., 32.
11. This bright young educated woman was a full-time religious worker in the campus ministry. She was the one previously mentioned who lost her faith at one point but returned to Christianity not through the reading of the Scriptures but through the poetry of T. S. Eliot. Biblical truths in modern literature!
12. DeWire, op. cit., 133–140.
13. DeWire, op. cit., 184.
14. DeWire, op. cit., 64.
15. I once heard several young people presenting their canned approach to a high school girl at Lake Tahoe. They went through their routine, and then asked, "You accept this, don't you?" The girl quietly replied, "No, not at all." Similarly, a Florida pastor's wife answered her front door and was confronted by a girl who asked, "Are you saved?" "Yes," replied the woman, "don't we have a wonderful Savior?" "You *are*?" the girl responded with a downcast look on her face. She had lost her chance to "up the body count" one more. Particularly repellent are those Dale Carnegie strategies that advise you to praise the person's athletic trophy for five minutes and then "move in for the kill." Walk softly, but carry a big Bible. Or, keep a small New Testament in your pocket, and at the right time you can draw it out and "shoot 'em *alive.*"
16. I once tried to witness to a realtor whose baby had died. His first response was, "Where do you think the Indians came from?"
17. Hale, op. cit., 91.
18. See "The Ministry of Listening" by Dietrich Bonhoeffer in *Life Together* (N.Y.: Harper & Row, 1954), 97–99.
19. DeWire, op. cit., 71.
20. A frustrated non-Christian once said to his Christian friend, "Why is it that every time I ask you a question, you answer with a question?" To which the Christian replied, "Why not?"
21. DeWire, op. cit., 74.
22. Halford Luccock, in *The Christian Century*, Vol. 72 (1955), 360.
23. Donald L. Deffner, *You Say You're Depressed?* (Nashville: Abingdon, 1973), 17.
24. Always listen very carefully to the last words people say as they leave your door. They may just drop a clue as to the real reason for coming to see you
25. DeWire, op. cit., 77. Some might add except with relatives." We are often inhibited in our witness to those nearest and dearest to us. They know us so well—our weaknesses, our foibles, our inconsistencies in what we *say* as Christians in contrast to the way we often *live.* Sometimes all we can do is trust that

the Holy Spirit will give us the grace to *live as a Christian* with our family and pray that someone else may be a better "little Christ" to those of our kin who do not yet know the Lord.

26. A woman once wrote to Dr. Walter A. Maier of the International Lutheran Hour saying she had been praying for 35 years that her unbelieving husband might become a Christian, but she was about to give up. What should she do? Dr. Maier wrote back, "Keep praying. Perhaps in the 36th year . . ."
27. Joost A. M. Merloo, *Conversation and Communication*, (Madison, CT: International Universities Press, 1952), 135.
28. DeWire, op. cit., 78.
29. Exception: A young man once visited my parish and said the reason he was interested in Christianity was a student who lived in the same boarding house he did. "That man has a *faith to live by,*" he said. "I want that faith." My point here is grace-filled Christian living *and* verbal witness to Christ are both vital.
30. Matt. 10:19; Acts 17:18; cf. Philip and the Ethopian eunuch, Acts 8:34ff.
31. Mark 10:21. See also Mark 1:41. The Greek verb used here to denote Jesus' condition of deep sympathy is *splagkhnistheis*. The Nestle text of the Greek at Matt. 9:36 lists the many parallel uses of this word. In its various forms (used twelve times in the gospels) this verb always denotes Jesus' vicarious compassion, treating the victim as if the sin or sickness were our Lord's very own. It is not used of the sympathy of Christians toward other people. (In the parable of the Prodigal Son, Luke 15, it pictures the compassion of God toward the repentant sinner.) We can sympathize but we cannot have compassion in the sense in which Jesus did, because we cannot vicariously take to ourselves the sins and sickness of mankind the way Jesus did." Harold H. Buls, *Exegetical Notes, Gospel Notes*, Series B, Mark–John, Festival Season Sundays (Fort Wayne: Concordia Theological Seminary Press, 1981), 43.
32. DeWire, op. cit., 97.
33. A cherry-blonde graduate student in chemistry once walked into our chapel in Berkeley and said to a student, "I'm an atheist. Argue with me." The student said, "We don't argue with anyone around here. Come on in." She did. She stayed for three years, even sang in the chapel choir. She never became a Christian, but before she left she told me, "You know, Pastor Don, the 'hound of heaven' may get me yet."
34. DeWire, op. cit., 99.
35. A young pastor left his first parish after three years and returned to the seminary for advanced study. He told me that before he left he had just confirmed a man. But when the pastor announced he was leaving, the man said, "Oh, Pastor, you can't do this to me!" The pastor was afraid the man had joined the pastor rather than joining the church, so close the relationship had become. But he was happily proved wrong.
36. Peter A. Bertocci, "What Makes a Christian Home?" *The Christian Century*, LXXVI, 18, (May 1959).
37. Padovano, op. cit., 166. Strictly speaking, love can have a useful purpose, also for the person showing love; but the less the person expects results, the more selfless and effective it may be.
38. I remember a woman in a church basement pointing proudly to certain persons painting the walls. "Those are the active ones!" she kept repeating. She inti-

mated that they were more spiritual than those who had stayed home. But who knows and who decides whether a certain father serves better in the church basement rather than as "the priest in the house in the church in the home?" The notion of the *Super-Christian* can also be a deterrent to the opening of dialog with non-Christian neighbors. One woman described a couple who were at their church "four nights a week and all day Sunday"—and who made quite a point of it to their unchurched friends. With due respect for their involvement in the (institutional) church, one wonders how much time might better be spent *listening* to their neighbors—late at night after the barbecue fires have burned out—and hear their haunted *whys* about life and death.

39. No source given except from "Old J. R. Miller (1840-1912)" as quoted in Jard DeVille, *The Psychology of Witnessing* (Waco: Word Books, 1980), 125.
40. Bonhoeffer, op. cit., 35–36.
41. Ibid.

References

Andersen, Richard, and Donald L. Deffner. *For Example: Illustrations for Contemporary Preaching*. St. Louis: Concordia Publishing House, 1977.

Anderson, G., and T. Stransky, eds. *Evangelization: Missions Trends #2*. New York: Paulist Press, 1975.

Camus, Albert. *The Fall*. New York: Alfred A. Knopf, 1958.

———. *The Plague*. New York: Modern Library, 1948.

Deffner, Donald L. *A Primer/Primer for Preachers*. Ft. Wayne: Concordia Theological Seminary Press, 1988.

———, ed. *Toward Adult Christian Education*. River Forest, IL: 19th Yearbook of the Lutheran Education Association, 1962.

DeWire, Harry E. *The Christian as Communicator*. Philadelphia: Westminster Press, 1961.

Diehl, William E. *Christianity and Real Life*. Philadelphia: Fortress Press, 1976.

Dittmer, Terry K., ed. *Wings of Faith: The Doctrines of the Lutheran Church for Teens*. St. Louis: Concordia Publishing House, 1988.

Gibson, Anthony. *The Silence of God*. New York: Harper and Row, 1969.

Greeley, Andrew. *The Cardinal Sins*. New York: Warner Books, 1984.

Griffin, Emory A. *The Mind Changers*. Wheaton: Tyndale House, 1982.

Hale, J. Russell. *Who Are the Unchurched?* Atlanta: Glenmary Research Center, 1977.

Kolb, Erwin J. *A Witness Primer*. St. Louis: Concordia Publishing House, 1986.

Kolb, Robert. *Speaking the Gospel Today*. St. Louis: Concordia Publishing House, 1987.

Lewis, C. S. *Mere Christianity*. New York: Macmillan, 1977.

———. *The Screwtape Letters*. New York: Macmillan, 1964.

Lewis, R. W. B. *The Picaresque Saint: Representative Figures in Contemporary Fiction*. New York: J. B. Lippincott, 1961.

Lischer, Richard. *Speaking of Jesus: Finding the Words for Witness*. Philadelphia: Fortress Press, 1982.

———. *A Theology of Preaching*. Nashville: Abingdon Press, 1981.

Mueller, William R. *The Prophetic Voice in Modern Fiction*. New York: Association Press, 1959.

Nederhood, Joel H., *The Church's Mission to the Educated American*. Grand Rapids: Wm. B. Eerdmans, 1960.

Newbigin, Lesslie. *Foolishness to the Greeks: The Gospel and Western Culture*. Grand Rapids: Wm. B. Eerdmans, 1986.

Padovano, Anthony. *The Estranged God: Modern Man's Search for Belief*. New York: Sheed and Ward, 1966.

Phillips, J. B. *God Our Contemporary*. New York: Macmillan, 1960.

Pippert, Rebecca M. *Out of the Salt Shaker: Evangelism as a Way of Life*. Downer's Grove: InterVarsity, 1979.

Powell, John. *A Reason to Live! A Reason to Die!* Niles: Argus Communications, 1975.

Rauff, Edward A. *Why People Join the Church*. New York: Pilgrim Press, 1980.

Roloff, Marvin L., ed. *Education for Christian Living*. Minneapolis: Augsburg, 1987.

Truemper, David G., and Frederick A., Niedner, Jr. *Keeping the Faith: A Guide to the Christian Message*. Philadelphia: Fortress Press, 1981.

Walsh, Chad. *Campus Gods on Trial*. New York: Macmillan, 1962.

Watkins, Morris. *The Great Commission*. Fullerton, CA: R. C. Law & Co., 1987.

Wiesel, Elie. *Night*. New York: Bantam Books, 1982.

The references above include books referred to in the manuscript and as such span several decades. Of special recent note is a work by David W. Gill, *The Opening of the Christian Mind* (Downer's Grove: InterVarsity Press, 1989). This is a strong, well-documented call for a spiritually educated laity and is highly recommended as a useful companion volume to *The Compassionate Mind*.

A list of "Contemporary Christian Novelists and Poets or Writers on Christian Themes" may be obtained by writing Karen L. Mulder, Christian in the Arts Networking, Inc., P.O. Box 1941, Cambridge, MA 02238-1941 or calling (617) 783–5667.